D1756769

As It Was

Sin Mar a Bha

An Ulva Boyhood

Donald W. MacKenzie

BIRLINN

*Dedicated
to the memory of
the last minister of Ulva,
my first Dominie,
my father;
and to the memory of
the Last Lady of the Manse of Ulva,
my first Alma mater,
my mother*

This edition first published in 2011 by
Birlinn Limited
West Newington House
10 Newington Road
Edinburgh EH9 1QS

© Donald W. MacKenzie 2000

All rights reserved.
No part of this publication may be reproduced, stored, or
transmitted in any form, or by any means,
electronic, photocopying, recording or other, without the
express written permission of the publisher.

ISBN 978 1 78027 010 4

British Library Cataloguing-in-Publication Data
A catalogue record for this book is available from the
British Library

Typeset by Textype, Cambridge
Printed and bound by CPI Antony Rowe,
Chippenham and Eastbourne

Contents

iv

Foreword

ULVA SUFFERED THE NEGLECT of public notice due to its proximity to Staffa and Iona. Visitors in the eighteenth and nineteenth centuries either bypassed Ulva or made it their stepping-off point on their tour of its more celebrated neighbours. Sir Joseph Banks visited Staffa in 1772 and when his description of it was published in Pennant's *A Tour in Scotland and Voyage to the Hebrides* visitors flocked to see the wonders of Staffa for themselves, a fact that called forth the disgruntled comment of a writer: 'As long as the mass of mankind is content to follow the individual that first led the way, so long will the beauties of Ulva be consigned to popular neglect.'

The best known tourists in the eighteenth century, Dr Samuel Johnson and James Boswell, landed on Ulva by accident and left it the following morning to resume their planned itinerary to Staffa and Iona via Inch Kenneth because Boswell, as he recorded later, had learned that the island contained nothing worthy of exploration. It is to Dr Johnson's credit that, in that short visit, he was able to discern, beyond the chief's mean dwelling, the nobility of the chief himself and to appreciate the tragedy of his impending dispossession of his ancestral lands.

Nearly all the visitors to Ulva, like Johnson and Boswell, were unable to understand the language spoken by the people and they gained all their impressions of them from the English-speaking inhabitants with whom they lodged and conversed – the landowners, gentry and ministers. From the diaries and journals they wrote we learn next to nothing about the native population, their beliefs, customs or culture. It comes as a pleasant surprise, therefore, to come across the account of a visitor who spent the most part of a month in the summer of 1800 in Ulva. She was Mrs S. Murray of Kensington, the redoubtable traveller who wrote *A Companion and Useful Guide*. She remarked that 'Ulva was so often unheeded by gentlemen of taste and mineralogical science because of lack of time'. She was the guest of the widow of Colin MacDonald of Boisdale and her son, Ranald, who succeeded his father that year. 'I was so greatly amused at Ulva House', she wrote, 'that I do not remember twenty-six days ever seemed to pass so quickly.' It was not the MacDonald household only that engaged her lively interest. She observed the islanders as they thronged around the doors seeking help and advice from the new laird's mother, whom they regarded as the Mother of the People. She visited and describes a humble cottage; she watched the women waulking tweed, using hands and feet; she listened with pleasure to their singing and saw them dancing; she appreciated the important place that music and song occupied in their way of life. On long rambles through the island she collected geological specimens, 'fossils, crystals of zeolite porphyry and spar'. (Eve Eckstein, *Visitors to Mull*)

The most detailed and glowing description of Ulva and its people was written by one who was living in the island and who took the trouble to learn Gaelic. He not only lived in Ulva: he also owned it. He was Francis William Clark, who bought the island in 1835 and drew up the account of the parish for the New Statistical Account of 1843. It is one of the most bitter ironies of fate that it was this same man who, a few years later, began the process of evictions which ultimately reduced the population to a handful of people.

The story of Ulva and its people goes back a long way. Recent archaeological excavations in the floor of the cave we knew as Livingstone's cave have uncovered shell heaps, flint implements and fragments of bone – lemming, Arctic fox and human – that provide the only evidence of the people who inhabited Ulva about 5650 BC and the two standing stones on the south side near Cragaig and the single one near the ruins of the old school are the only memorials of the pre-Celtic megalithic people who flourished around 1500 BC.

Ulva is a microcosm of the Western Isles which once formed a kingdom distinct from the kingdoms of mainland Scotland. We tend to think of islands like Ulva as remote and inaccessible because they are sea-girt. In earlier times the sea itself was an open highway that linked, rather than separated, islands and even continents together. It was by sea that the early colonists, the Scots, came who were to give the whole country its name and most of the inhabitants their language, Gaelic. Kuno Meyer's oft quoted saying is an affirmation of the Irish origin of the Scots: 'No Scot set his foot on British soil save from a vessel that had put out from Ireland.'

By c. AD 500 these Gaelic-speaking colonists from Ireland, the Scots, were well established in Dalriada (Dál

Riata), so named after the territory in the north of Ireland they came from, and by the mid seventh century Dalriada included Islay, Mull, Tiree, Coll, Colonsay, Gigha, Bute and Arran and the mainland areas of Argyll, Kintyre, Cowal, Lòrn and Ardnamurchan. The name Argyll is from the Irish Airir Goidel (Oirthir Ghaidheal – 'Coastline of the Gaels'). Ultimately the whole of the Western Isles and the western coastline of the mainland formed the kingdom of the King of the Scots and in AD 843 the kingdoms of the Scots and of the Picts were united under Kenneth MacAlpine, the King of the Scots. At some time during the Irish colonisation of Scotland there arrived from Ireland a person of royal descent named Guaire, the eponymous ancestor of the MacQuarries of Ulva.

Early on, too, in the course of the colonisation, Columba (Colum Cille – 'Dove of the Churches'), a Gaelic-speaking monk of royal birth, set out in a coracle from Ireland with twelve companions and founded c. AD 563 his monastery in Iona – I Colum Cille. Iona was chosen not because it was remote and isolated but because it was a centre from which the surrounding islands and the mainland coast were readily accessible by sea for missionary enterprises. The Telford church of Ulva was not the first Christian place of worship on the island: the first church was dedicated to St Ewan of Ardstraw who was a nephew of St Columba. The burial ground at Cill Mhic Eoghain on the South Side commemorates his name. Nearby Inch Kenneth is named after Canice (Coinneach), a contemporary of St Columba who worked in the Western Isles including Inch Kenneth. He founded a monastery at Aghaboe in Ossory. Another contemporary was Comgall (AD 517–603), Abbot of Bangor monastery, one of the principal Irish monasteries.

Two of his monks, St Moluag of Lismore and St Mael-Rubha of Applecross are among the most revered of the Celtic saints and their names are enshrined in many place-names. Comgall lived in a monastery in Tiree. Both Canice and Comgall were Irish Picts who accompanied St Columba on his missionary expedition to King Brude, king of the northern Picts at Inverness. It has been suggested that they were chosen because, as speakers of the Pictish language, they would facilitate communication between the Gaelic-speaking Celt, St Columba and the Pictish-speaking Celt, King Brude.

From the eighth century the islands were threatened by other sea-borne invaders – the Vikings from Scandinavia. In AD 795 Iona was sacked and from AD 800 until 1266 the islands were settled by the Norsemen. The Hebrides are still called in Gaelic Innse Ghall – 'the Islands of the Foreigners'. They colonised the Northern Isles, Orkney and Shetland (the Nordreys) and the Western Isles as far south as the Isle of Man (the Sudreys). One of the most abiding legacies of their occupation is to be found in place-names: Ulva is the Old Norse *Ulfr + ey* – Wolf Island, Wolf probably a personal name; Gometra was Godman's Island; Eorsa, probably Eors Island; Ormaig is O.N. *orm + vik* – Serpent Bay; Oskamull, O.N. *Oska + muli* – Oska's Peninsula. There are many hybrid, Old Norse/Gaelic names: Eas Fors – Gaelic *eas* – waterfall + O.N. *fors* – waterfall; Carn Burg – Gaelic *carn* – heap of stones + O.N. *borgr* – fortified place; Corkamull – Gaelic *Coirce* – oats + *muli* – ridge or peninsula. On the top of a small conical islet, Dùn Bàn, between Ulva and Gometra, there is a fortified dwelling of the Norse period, Glacindaline Castle.

The Norse occupation ended in 1266 when, by the Treaty of Perth, Norway ceded the sovereignty of the

Isles to Scotland. The Norse dominance in the Isles had been challenged successfully long before the formal treaty by the kings of Scotland, Alexander II, and his son, Alexander III. The latter fought off King Hakon's raiding forces at the battle of Largs in 1263, and the old King of Norway died in Orkney on his way home. It is said that a MacQuarrie took part in this battle on the side of the Scottish king. MacQuarries also supported Robert the Bruce and fought at Bannockburn in 1314. In Argyll and the Isles another royal dynasty was being established and extending its influence in the west. In 1150 the Norse/Gaelic King Somerled had wrested the Western Isles from Norway and he and his descendants, the Lords of the Isles, or Kings of the Isles, re-established the Gaelic rule of the former Dalriadic kingdom. From 1354 to 1493 the Isles were governed by them independent on the kings of Scotland. The first of these lords, Good John of Islay, controlled the whole of the Hebrides from Islay to Lewis except Skye. The MacQuarries supported the Lords of the Isles and their chiefs were members of the Council of the Isles that determined the policies of government in war and peace.

After the forfeiture of the Lordship, the MacQuarries followed and supported the powerful Clan Maclean. Their chief, Alan MacQuarrie, died at the battle of Inverkeithing in 1651 along with Hector Maclean of Duart. Men of Ulva fought at Culloden and a grandson of the last MacQuarrie of Ulva fell at Waterloo. After the break-up of the clan system the Isles entered into the period of the 'New Men', a period of transition from chiefs to landlords, the time of the kelp boom and failure of the potato famine, of the evictions and emigrations.

Ulva has a long history and had an important place in the history of Scotland. Its history has yet to be written. I lived in Ulva from 1918, when I was just over a year old until 1929, when I was about twelve. I am the only person now alive who lived continuously in Ulva during these eleven inter-war years – a kind of Indian summer in the island's history. In this book I have set down some of the things I remember from these years; what I saw and heard and experienced and was told; the trivia and commonplaces of everyday life; the tasks and pastimes; what the people said and did and how they lived. Over the years I have been comparing my memories with those of my contemporaries and I have been reading newspaper articles, news items, Letters to the Editor contributed to the *Oban Times* and other papers, many of them written by my father and retained in a scrapbook which I still have. Other sources of information include Statistical Accounts, the Fasti of the Church of Scotland, the Report of the Commissioners for Building Churches in the Highlands, rent rolls and state papers and, of course, magazine articles and books about Mull, many of them published within the last ten to fifteen years, from all of which I have extracted the meagre references to Ulva and its people, and which has helped to fill the gaps in my memories or to reinforce or correct my personal impressions.

My 'story' of Ulva is a very small fragment, a tiny piece of a very large historical jigsaw puzzle. It has been my aim to present the Ulva that I knew as a real place; not just a grid reference on a map; as a living community of people; not just a collection of statistics. I hope that those who read this book will feel that they have visited a real island and that they have met the real men, women and children who once lived there.

Acknowledgments

I T IS WITH A sense of indebtedness and of gratitude that I record the names of many persons without whose help this book would be sadly inadequate. Many of then are no longer with us and my acknowledgement of their contribution is by way of adding a stone on the cairn of their remembrance – clach eile air a' chàrn.

It has been my privilege, over the years, to have listened to some of the best tradition-bearers and informants of Mull, including Lachie Maclean, Knock; the late Donald Morrison, Ross of Mull; the late Angie Henderson, Tobermory and the late Mary Morrison, Mornish, whose brother, the Rev. Alex D. MacRae, was minister of Salen, the parish with which Ulva was united after 1929. The Gaelic title of the book, *Sin Mar a Bha*, is borrowed from Donald Morrison, who often used the phrase to round off a story before beginning on another.

Through the years, after leaving Ulva, I have had occasional contacts with people who, like myself, once lived there and now lived elsewhere – Roddie MacNeill, Salen; Colin Fletcher, Craignure; Mrs Donald MacFarlane (née Tina Fletcher), Deargphort and Lachie MacNeill (Lachie Beag), Acharoinich – who have shared with me their memories of life in Ulva and Ulvaferry, sometimes corroborating, sometimes correcting and sometimes adding to those of mine. Others who had links with Ulva, the late Johnny Simpson and Chrissie MacDonald, Fanmore, have also passed on information that has been useful and interesting.

I am indebted to the Hon Mrs Jean D. Howard, the present proprietor of Ulva, for graciously granting me permission to publish material from the Estate Papers, and to her son, Jamie Howard, and Anne Jones, co-authors of *The Isle of Ulva, A Visitor's Guide*, and to Donald Munro for making available to my daughter, Ann, copies of papers and pictures for inclusion in the book.

A special word of thanks is due to my daughter Ann (C. Ann MacKenzie), who has been living in Mull for the past eight years and without whose assistance this book might not have been completed. She has had many contacts with the people of North Mull and has recorded many of them on tape. She has located published and unpublished material and made it available for publication. She has also provided a selection of photographs taken by her in Ulva included in this book.

I am grateful to all the authors and publishers who have so willingly given me permission to quote from their works which are listed in the Bibliography. All such quotations and references are duly acknowledged and attributed in the text.

While I have pleasure in acknowledging my indebtedness to all of these, I take full responsibility for any factual errors or misinterpretation of the facts that may occur. I do not seek to evade such responsibility by using the old traditional Gaelic disclaimer – 'Ma's breug bhuams' i 'si breug dhomhs' i' ('If an untruth has come from me it is an untruth that came to me').

Donald W. MacKenzie   Perth
                                                      April 2000

Preface

THE FIRST WORLD WAR had still five months of its
bloody course to run before it ended in the Armistice
signed at the eleventh hour of the eleventh day of the
eleventh month of 1918, when a small procession made
its way along the winding track from the island pier to
the manse about a mile distant. The warm summer air
was scented with the bog-myrtle which grew in profusion
on either side and with the wild thyme which grew
between the cart-wheel ruts on the track. As it skirted the
tidal inlets the pungent tang of sea and seaweed sharpened the scent of the air.

Leading the procession, accompanied by an elder, was
the new minister of the island, fifty-four years of age and
portly in build. Although the afternoon was warm and
sunny he wore a long black coat, and his hat was set well
down on his head, its brim shielding his face from the
sun's rays which he, like most country people of the time,
believed to be harmful to the skin. In one hand he carried
a small Gladstone bag and in the other an umbrella, more

by way of a status symbol than for its practical use.

As the dusty grass-grown track was too narrow to accommodate more than two persons walking abreast, the minister's wife, twenty years his junior, followed a few yards behind him. She, too, was accompanied by a member of the congregation, and she pushed in front of herself a folding, wood and canvas contraption, mounted on wheels – the 'go-cart' – in which her infant son was ensconsed.

Taking up the rear of the procession were the other children of the family – a five-and-a-half year-old girl and a boy about four years old. Each carried a cardboard box, securely tied with cord, containing the family pets – a smokey-brown long-haired female cat called Percy and a small black cat without a tail. When later the island children saw the latter they thought that its tail had been docked in the same way that some dogs were docked. They had never seen a Manx cat before.

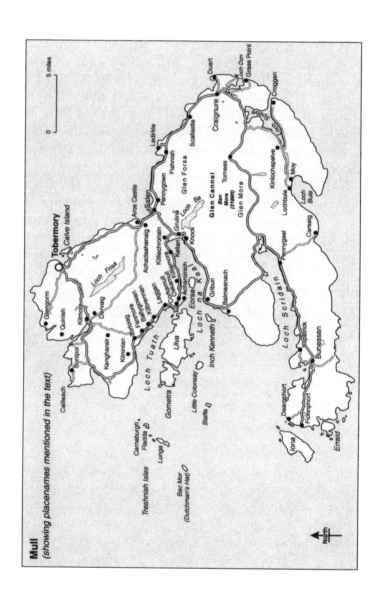

Mull
(showing placenames mentioned in the text)

0 _____ 5 miles

North

Glengorm
Quinish
Cailleach
Sunipol
Kilmore
Dervaig
Kengharair
Kilninian

Tobermory
Calve Island

Loch Frisa

Treshnish Isles
Carnaburgh
Fladda
Lunga

Bac Mor
(Dutchman's Hat)

Gometra
Ulva
Little Colonsay
Staffa

Achadashenaig
Killiechronain

Dhiseig
Fanmore
Ballygown
Kilbrenan
Lagan
Torloisk
Oskamull
Killiemore
Kellan
Kilfinichen
Acharonich

Loch Tuath

Eorsa

Loch na Keal

Gribun
Balmeanach

Inch Kenneth

Aros Castle
Salen
Pennygown
Gruline
Knock
Loch Ba

Glen Forsa

Fishnish
Ladirke
Scallastle
Craignure

Duart
Loch Don
Grass Point
Croggan

Glen Cannel
Ben More
(3169ft)
Torness
Glen More

Kinlochspelve
Lochbuie
Loch Buie
Moy

Loch Scridain

Pennygael
Carsaig

Kilpatrick
Bunessan

Deardghort
Fidhinphort

Iona
Erraid

Loch Spelve

1

A Brief Description of Ulva in Our Time

I MAY NOT HAVE A complete conscious recollection of
being pushed along in the 'go-cart' or of all the details I
have just set down – I was only fifteen months old at the
time – but I am pretty sure that that was how it was on
that June afternoon in 1918 when the family completed
the last stage of the long journey from Rothesay, Isle of
Bute, to Ulva, Isle of Mull. My father, Donald William
MacKenzie, after whom I was named, had been minister
of the Gaelic Church in Rothesay, and it was in Rothesay
that all the family were born. Four years after coming to
Ulva the family was completed by the birth, also in
Rothesay, of a fourth child, Roderick Stewart. Both my
father and mother were born in Lewis and were native
Gaelic speakers, but his parents and forebears belonged
to Harris. I still find it difficult to answer, in a single
word, or indeed in a single sentence, the simple question,
'Where do you come from?' There is a saying in Gaelic,
'Chan eil dùthchas aig mnaoi no aig ministear' ('A wife
or a minister has no birth-tie with any place'). When a

1

woman married she took her husband's surname and was adopted by his locality. Similarily, the priest or minister adopted the parish to which he was appointed as his 'duthchas'. The word for ordination in Gaelic is 'pòsadh' (marriage).

My father was the sixth and last of the ministers of the parish of Ulva, a parish which was created out of the parish of Kilninian some ninety years previously. When he was translated on 3rd December, 1929 to Kilninver and Kilmelford, Ulva was united with Salen, and the manse was no longer in use as a minister's residence. A hundred years of Ulva's ecclesiastical history then came to an end.

Of the five ministers who were my father's predecessors, two were unmarried and, in the official record of Church of Scotland ministers – the Fasti – the other three are not recorded as having families. Perhaps, then, we were the only children that were brought up in the manse during the hundred years of its occupation by the ministers of Ulva. I remember thinking, as a boy, that there could be no better place in which to spend one's childhood; eighty years on I have not found reason to revise that boyhood opinion. Mairi, Angus and Stewart would doubtless agree, but now I am the only member of the family left alive to tell the story of our Ulva years.

The island of Ulva, about five miles long from east to west and two and a half miles from north to south, is separated from the western mainland of Mull by Loch-a-tuath ('North Loch') and Loch na Keal (Loch nan Ceall – 'Loch of the Cells'), the two lochs linked by the Sound of Ulva (Caolas Ulbha) which, at its narrowest point where the ferry crosses, is about 300 yards wide. Numerous small islands, reefs and rocks lie around the coasts. Beinn Chreagach ('Rocky Ben'), 1027 ft, at roughly the middle of the central ridge, is the highest point in the island.

Situated about a mile west of the ferry, near the shores of Loch-a-tuath, were the church and manse whose fronts faced a little north of east, each within its own grounds enclosed by stone walls. At the north-west corner of the manse grounds stood a barn/byre with a corrugated iron roof. Between the manse grounds and the churchyard (which was not a place of burial) there was a walled garden with an old crab-apple tree in the middle. The glebe, also enclosed, extended eastward below the garden and manse grounds to the sea. The whole T-shaped area occupied by the complex extended to one and three-quarters of an acre of the Ardellum lands.

The church and its minister served the parish of Ulva, which included Ulva, Gometra (which had been linked to Ulva by a causeway early in the nineteenth century) and Little Colonsay. Staffa and the Treshnish Isles which lay within the boundaries of the parish were not inhabited in our time. Inch Kenneth and Eilean Eòrsa, also in Loch nan Ceall, belonged to the parish of the Ross of Mull. The coastal areas of the Mull mainland opposite Ulva from Acharoinich to Fanmore were also included in the parish of Ulva.

During our eleven years in Ulva the number of people living in the parish fluctuated around 120. During that period families left and others took their places; individuals left to get married, to study in schools, universities, colleges, to go to sea and so on, but I can remember and name about fifty of the people that lived across the ferry, about the same number of people living in Ulva, twenty or so in Gometra and one family, a shepherd and his two sons, who lived on Little Colonsay.

2

Why a Church Was Built on Ulva

IT DID NOT OCCUR to us as children, at first, to question why such a sparsely populated area as Ulva justified the building of a church there, but as we grew older and began exploring the countryside that lay beyond our cloistered domain we saw, everywhere we went, evidence that a large population had lived on the island in earlier times. We saw ruins of houses (tobhtaichean), roofless and windowless, and near them neglected green patches that had obviously been cultivated at one time. We saw overgrown ridges and furrows that had once been the lazy-beds (feannagan) on which former inhabitants had grown their potatoes and cereals. When we returned home after our explorations to recount our 'discoveries' we learned, over the years, that the Ulva of 1827, when the church and manse were built, was very different from the Ulva we came to know so well a hundred years later.

Commissioners for building Churches in the Highlands and Islands

Among the papers held by my father as parish minister was a typescript extract from 'The Sixth Report of the Commissioners for Building Churches in the Highlands of Scotland 1830–31', which gives a description of Ulva and the church and manse newly built there and which sets out the reasons why the site was chosen.

After the Battle of Waterloo in 1815, Britain, which had been engaged in warfare almost continuously for over fifty years, entered a period of peace, and the government of the time decided to erect churches in remote areas of Britain as an act of 'Thanksgiving for victory', in recognition of the sacrifice of so many lives during the years of conflict. An Act of Parliament in 1823, amended the following year, appointed a commission for building churches in the Highlands of Scotland as part of the National Programme.

The principal heritors were invited to apply to the commission for inclusion in the scheme and to provide the land for the churches, manses and glebes. The commissioners were to survey the areas, assess the needs, select the sites and prepare the plans. The costs of building and the provision of stipends were to be met by the Exchequer, and the ministers were to be presented by the Crown, hence the name parliamentary churches or chapels by which they were commonly known. Later, all the parliamentary parishes were erected Parishes Quoad Sacra, bringing them and their ministers within the polity of the Church of Scotland on equal terms with those of existing established parish churches.

Thomas Telford

The commissioners were men who already had hands-on experience of works of improvement in the Highlands and Islands, such as the Commission for Building Highland Roads and Bridges, the British Fisheries Society, the Caledonian and Crinan Canals. The chief surveyor or consulting engineer was Thomas Telford, the most highly acclaimed civil engineer of his time. William Thomson, the architect surveyor of the Crinan Canal, worked in close association with Telford and was the principal contractor on many of the building sites.

Of the forty-three sites in the Highlands and Islands finally agreed by the commissioners, five were in Mull – Iona, Kinlochspelvie, Tobermory, Salen and Ulva. In the case of Salen, instead of building a new church, a sum of money was provided to repair an existing church which was in ruins. Telford was closely involved in all five and Thomson was the principal contractor in them all. The Certificate of Completion of the Ulva church and manse is dated 14th March, 1828, the land conveyed by Charles MacQuarie, Esq., of Ulva. The total cost came to £1,495 14/1, falling neatly within the £1,500 limit imposed by the Act.

The major overhaul of the church in 1921

It is a tribute to the excellence of the design, material and workmanship that went into the building of Ulva's church that the first major overhaul was carried out in 1921, ninety-four years after its erection, when the roof was reslated and the exterior walls were reharled by the building contractors, Donald Fletcher and Co, Tobermory. I remember watching the men at work, skillfully dressing the slates and piercing the nail-holes in

them with their slaters' irons. I remember Alexander
Downie who was the foreman and a young man whose
name I do not recall but who was known by the nick-
name An Druid ('The Starling'). Another of the workers,
a MacCalman I think, had the distinction of having eyes
of different colours, one blue, the other brown. They
completed the work just before Christmas and on the last
day they were entertained at the manse, my mother
having prepared an extra large 'dumpling' to celebrate
the occasion.

Conditions in Ulva described in the report

The report describes the conditions prevailing in Ulva
and district which justified beyond question the
commissioners' decision to build the church where they
did. 'No district', they bluntly report, 'was more deficient
in the means of religious instruction than Ulva.' The
district which included Ulva, Gometra, Staffa, Little
Colonsay and part of the mainland of Mull formed part
of the parish of Kilninian, which had been united under
one minister with the parish of Kilmore in 1628.

The commissioners in their report give the population
of Kilmore as 2,750 and that of Kilninian as 4,357, of
which 900 lived in the district of Ulva. The minister
preached on alternate Sundays in the two churches,
Kilmore and Kilninian, both built in 1754, and which
were about eight miles apart. Some of the parishioners
lived as much as twelve miles from the nearest and, since
the district was divided by rivers, lochs and mountains,
and the roads were so defective, it was not surprising that
'Divine Service was little frequented particularly in
Winter.'

The minister had commitments to the developing

villages of Tobermory and Salen, with some assistance from lay missionaries. 'He visited the island of Ulva four times a year, if the weather and other circumstances permitted, to administer the rites of Baptism and Marriage. Latterly a lay missionary preached once a fortnight in the open air with sometimes a blanket or sail spread to shelter him. The attendance was limited and irregular.'

The report notes that the natives were engaged in farming, fishing and the manufacture of kelp. The young men migrated in autumn to the south for employment at the harvest. They are described as 'peaceable, honest and industrious'.

3

The MacQuarries of Ulva

IT WOULD BE IMPOSSIBLE to grow up in Ulva without being aware of the important place occupied by the MacQuarries in the island's history or, indeed, in the country's history during the nine hundred years they were reputed to have been associated with Ulva. Although the clan was small, as was the territory they occupied, the MacQuarrie chiefs sat alongside those of the major clans in the Council of the Isles in the days of the Lords of the Isles (or Kings of the Isles, as they styled themselves) and their names appear on record from the fifteenth century in connection with affairs of State in times of peace and war. They were of Irish origin and claimed kinship with the kings of Ireland and Scotland.

MacQuarrie is now the accepted spelling of the clan name in Mull but MacQuarie is the preferred spelling of the name in Australia. The Gaelic spelling has long been standardised as MacGuaire. The names of the chiefs that appear on record are spelled in a bewildering variety of ways, perhaps that of a sixteenth century chief is the most bizarre. His name in Gaelic would be Donnsleibhe MacGuaire, Ulbha, but it appears variously as: Dunslavie McVoirich, Dulleis MaKwiddy of Ulua, Dwnsleif MaKcurra, Dwnsleyf MaKwra of Ulway. The personal name Dunslav from the Irish Donn-sleibhe (meaning 'Prince of the Hill') was common in Ireland and Scotland and, according to Jo Currie (*Mull Family Names*) it was still on record in Ulva in 1693. The surname derived from it is MacDhuinshleibhe, anglicised Livingstone. Neil Livingstone, the father of David Livingstone, the famous explorer/missionary was born in Ulva and was known in Mull as Niall Beag MacDhuin-shleibhe.

On one of our excursions Angus and I explored the old dilapidated farm buildings about a quarter of a mile from the laird's house. When we returned home we were told that we had been at the site of the last MacQuarrie chief's house, part of whose walls had been incorporated into the farm steadings. It was there, we were told, that the old and last chief, Lachlan MacQuarrie XVI, entertained two unexpected guests one wet, stormy night in October 1773 – a Dr Samuel Johnson, who 'wrote a dictionary' and a Mr James Boswell, who 'wrote a journal'.

They both recorded their impressions of their night's stay on Ulva. They were agreeably surprised by the appearance and character of their hospitable host whom they found to be 'intelligent, polite and much a man of the world'. But they were not favourably impressed by the mean house in which he lived, especially by the room in which they slept, whose earthern floor was soaked with the rain driven in through a broken window pane. They left the following morning for Inch Kenneth to continue their journey to Iona without further exploration of Ulva.

Dr Johnson realised that MacQuarrie's predicament

was due to his extravagance and negligence and he wrote, 'I saw with grief the chief of a very ancient clan, whose island was condemned by law to be sold for the satisfaction of his creditors.' Later, when he heard of the sale of Ulva to Captain Dugald Campbell of Achnaba in 1777, he wrote, 'Every eye must look with pain on a Campbell turning the MacQuarries at will out of their *sedes avitae*, their hereditary island.'

An article on Ulva contributed by my father to the *Oban Times* in January 1922 contains notes on the MacQuarries of Ulva which provide a sort of melancholy epitaph for the last chief of the clan, Lachlan MacQuarrie. His eldest daughter, Marie, married Gillean Maclaine of Scallastle, a son of Murdoch Maclaine of Loch Buidhe. They had a family of twelve children, four sons of whom had distinguished careers in the army: General Archibald, Colonel Hector, Murdoch, killed at the battle of Maida in 1806, and John, killed at Waterloo in 1815. Their mother, Marie, was presented with a medal by King George IV. Inscribed on it were the words 'Màthair nan Gaisgeach' – 'The Mother of the Heroes'.

Included in the article there is a letter, dated 5th October 1817, written by her three daughters, Flora, Mary and Margaret Ann, Lederkle Cottage (Fishnish). It is a plea addressed to Lord Palmerston, at that time Junior Lord of the Admiralty and Secretary for War:

'Our mother', they write, 'is at present attending the sickbed of an expiring parent, a venerable chieftain, originally from Ireland. He was once blessed with one and twenty sons, none of whom remain to lay his head in the grave.' Four of the brave young men fell in India fighting for King and Country, leaving no relatives save the three young ladies who 'had uncles who died as Generals and left none behind them but us three'. Their own brave brothers left neither widows no orphans.

Lachlan MacQuarrie, the sixteenth and last chief of the Clan MacQuarrie, lived for forty-one years after selling his ancestral lands. These latter years of his life have been fully documented by R.W. Munro, the eminent authority on the clan, in his book *Lachlan MacQuarrie XVI of Ulva*, on which I base this brief summary to round off this chapter.

During the American War of Independence, MacQuarrie enlisted in the Argyll Highlanders, his commission as a lieutenant dating from 1777, the year Ulva was sold, when he was sixty-three years old, and he saw action in Nova Scotia and Penobscot, Maine. The regiment was disbanded in 1783 and he was retired on half pay. He lived in straitened circumstances on Little Colonsay, 'cold Griban', and latterly in a house provided by Charles MacQuarrie of Glen Forsa (later, of Ulva) at Pennygowan where he died, reputedly one hundred and three years old, on 14th January, 1818. It was his wish that he should be buried in Iona beside his illustrious ancestors, 'M'Guare and lynages and the best men of all the Iles' (Sir Donald Monro). Bad weather denied him his wish and he was buried in Inch Kenneth where his father, John, the fifteenth chief, had been laid to rest eighty-three years previously.

4

Fifty Years of the 'New Men'
1777–1827

THE MACQUARRIE LANDS WERE put up for sale by public roup in Edinburgh in July 1777 and were bought by Captain Dugald Campbell of Achnaba for £9,080. From that time up to 1827, when the church was built in Ulva, covers a period of fifty years of the 'new men', so called because they had no ancestral or territorial connections with the island – some of them were Lowlanders – but also new in the sense that their concept of ownership and their relationship to their tenants were very different from those of the old hereditary chiefs under the clan system. The first fifty years of these 'new men' were to witness changes in the island life that even the wildest leaps of Boswell's imagination could not have envisaged.

In the public notice of the sale, Ulva was described as being 'almost in the state of nature' but was capable of much improvement. That description could apply to most of Mull at the same period. Nine years before Johnson and Boswell visited Ulva the island was visited

by the Rev. [later Dr] John Walker. He had been com-
missioned by the Commissioners of Annexed Estates and
had been instructed by the Church of Scotland and the
Scottish Society for the Propagation of Christian
Knowledge to report on the state of religion and
education in the Highlands and Islands. The Rev. Dr
John Walker's *Report on the Hebrides of 1764 and 1771*,
edited by Margaret M. McKay, Edinburgh, 1980 is the
source on which the following brief account of Mull in
the second half of the eighteenth century is based.

Walker visited Ulva in 1764 and noted that its
population was 266 with a rental value of £200, that of
Gometra was fifty with a rental value of £40. The total
population of Mull was 5,325, with evidence that it was
less populated than formerly. He gives three main reasons
for the depopulation:

1 'The high martial Spirit of the People has drained the
   Country on all warlike Occasions'
2 'The easy Access to the South was drawing away the
   Inhabitants'
3 'The pernicious Emigration of great Numbers to
   Ireland'.

Mull, which we celebrated in song as 'Mull of the Trees'
('Muile nan Craobh'), he found, like Dr Johnson, to be
destitute of trees. Sheep rearing had become unprofitable
owing to the devastation among flocks caused by eagles
and foxes, especially foxes which had increased in numbers as a result of the disarming of Highlanders. Tenants
were able to keep only sufficient sheep to clothe their
families, and were obliged to breed, instead, large numbers of goats which, though less profitable, were 'better
armed and of greater courage than sheep and lay where
the fox dare not attack them'. Walker recommends that

half a dozen men in each parish be armed to combat the fox menace. Alternatively, the fox could be hunted with dogs, a suitable pack, he suggests, might consist of 'three Grey Hounds, three Terriers, two couples of Strong Beagles'.

Although herring, cod and ling were plentiful around the coasts, there was 'no Net or Long Line on the island to catch them and none of the Inhabitants were acquainted with any kind of Fishing but with the Rod from Sea Rocks'.

Walker is critical of the landlords and tacksmen for granting short term leases and for exacting excessive service from their sub-tenants one day of the week of their labour throughout the year. Neglect of tillage resulted in the land becoming overgrown with heath.

Twenty-eight years after Walker visited Ulva, the Rev. Archibald McArthur, minister of the parish of Kilninian, of which Ulva formed a part, compiled the account of his parish which is included in the *Old Statistical Account*, 1792–93. He records some improvements in housing, the development of Tobermory and progress in ground enclosure but he is critical of the landowners for their pursuit of short-term profits for their families to the neglect of the welfare of their tenants. He deplores the short leases, the frequent removals, the frequent augmentation of rent, the frequent checks on improvement and the abject state of dependence in which tenants were held.

He concludes with the gloomy prediction: 'There seems very little ground to hope for a speedy increase of its population or prosperity, but rather the reverse.' Events were taking place, however, even as he wrote, that would shortly prove his pessimistic forecast dramatically wrong, at least as far as Ulva was concerned and, at least for a limited period.

Warfare, emigration abroad, migration to the south, kelp manufacture, potato growing, the introduction of Lowland sheep to the islands, all of which are mentioned in the Walker and McArthur reports, are the strands that are interwoven in the fabric of Ulva's history during the years of the 'New Men'.

5

The High Martial Spirit on all Warlike Occasions

B RITAIN WAS INVOLVED IN warfare almost continuously throughout the second half of the eighteenth century and into the nineteenth century. During the Seven Years' War (1756–63), of the 350 Mull men who served in the army, fifty returned. A great many were killed in America 'and the rest are still in service' according to Walker. During that war, Pitt, the Elder, raised a number of fighting regiments from clans and territories that were formerly Jacobite. His oft quoted dictum was a source of pride to every Highland schoolboy: 'I sought for merit wherever it was to be found. It is my boast that I was the first who looked for it in the mountains of the North. I called it forth and drew into your service a hardy and intrepid race of men . . . they served with fidelity as they fought with valour, and conquered for you in every part of the world.'

The pride we took in those glowing words might have been somewhat deflated had we known that Pitt had commended to 'Lord Hardwicke his decision on other grounds, namely that not many of them would return.' Thus his policy served a double purpose. It provided King George II and his heirs with some of the finest soldiers in the world. And at the same time it denuded the Highlands of manpower and so removed a potential threat to the House of Hanover.' (Fitzroy Maclean, *A Concise History of Scotland*).

Our heroes were the generals and admirals we read about in our readers and history books – Horatio Nelson, celebrated in Thomas Campbell's poem, 'Of Nelson and the North Sing the Glorious Day's Renown', General James Wolfe, the victor in the battle of Quebec in 1759 in which he was killed. I learned later that James Wolfe had fought at Culloden on the Hanovarian side and that afterwards he had put forward a plan to exterminate the Highlanders on some flimsy pretext. Telling of this plan in a letter he added the remark 'Would you believe that I am so bloody? But 'twas my real intention.'

The Glasgow-born Sir John Moore who was killed at the battle of Corunna in 1809 during the Peninsular War, another hero, had no anti-Highlander agenda as far as I know. When one of my toy lead soldiers became a battle casualty beyond repair he was given a burial like Sir John's as described so touchingly by the poet Charles Wolfe that I read in my reader:

Not a drum was beat, not a funeral note,
As his corse to the rampart we hurried;
Not a soldier discharged his farewell shot
O'er the grave where our hero was buried.

No useless coffin enclosed his breast,
Not in sheet or in shroud we wound him;
But he lay like a warrior taking his rest
With his martial cloak around him.

The history we learned from our readers and history books was intended to inculcate in us a patriotic pride in Britain and her glorious Empire on which 'the sun never set'. On the walls of classrooms in little schools all over the islands hung maps of the world showing the British possessions abroad coloured red, and little boys and girls, just beginning to learn English, were taught to take pride in their ancestors who gave their lives in the empire-building.

The army offered new careers to the young men of the islands and many of them, including MacQuarries of Ulva, attained high rank and gave distinguished service in many theatres of war throughout the world. As Pitt predicted, however, not many of them were to return. But the conquests of war extended the range of overseas colonies and prospects were opening up in Canada, India and Australia for the young and able scions of the old clans.

One of the most successful and famous of the colonisers was an Ulva man, Lachlan MacQuarie (he spelled his name with one 'r'), an older brother of Charles MacQuarie, who owned Ulva from 1825 to 1835. It is not known who their father was or where they were born, but it is generally assumed that they were members of the Ormaig branch of the clan, the senior cadet branch of the MacQuarries of Ulva. Their mother, Margaret, was a sister of Murdoch Maclaine of Lochbuie and Margaret's mother was a half-sister of the fifteenth MacQuarrie chief.

Lachlan was born in 1761 and Lagganulva, Oskamull and Ulva itself have been variously suggested as his birthplace. In the archives of the Isle of Mull museum there is a letter, dated 29th July 1939, written by John MacGillivray, Balmeanach, Gribun, Mull, to a Mr

Morrison which contains the following passage:

> There are different opinions as to where G.
> [General] MacQuarrie was born. Old John
> MacQuarrie said he was born near the present
> Fank. I remember having talk with you on this
> subject some time ago and you told [me] a certain
> lady whose father was a schoolmaster in Ulva said
> G. MacQuarrie was born at Culagheata. G.
> MacQuarrie once brought home a Big Englishman
> with him and they went for a walk down to
> Culagheata. MacQuarrie ask[ed] the Englishman
> What would you think of a man that was born in
> one of these little Houses or huts? The Englishman
> replied He could not be up to much. G. MacQuarrie
> said, 'It's there I was born.' Probably this lady
> would be Mrs MacDonald . . . MacQuarrie must
> have been a very clever man. He got on in the world.
> I understand he was a poor man's son but he must
> have got Good Schooling. You will remember they
> never managed settle who his father was.

The writer of the letter was possibly John MacGillivray who was manager of the Ulva estate until 1919 when he left and went to Balemeanach. The Mr Morrison to whom it was addressed may have been one of the Morrisons of Kengharair who were well-versed in the history and traditions of Mull families. I cannot identify 'old John MacQuarrie' or the Mrs MacDonald mentioned in the letter. The place Cùl a' Gheata ('Back of the Gate') is about a quarter of a mile south of Ulva House.

Although Lachlan was not a direct descendant of the last MacQuarrie chief, he appears to have assumed as of right the headship of the clan without claiming the title. It was his brother Charles who provided a home at Pennygowan on his estate of Glenforsa for the aged chief during his latter years and Lachlan offered to contribute towards the cost of his upkeep there (R.W. Munro). In a genealogical and biographical record of the MacDonalds of Carey's Ranges, published in Melbourne, there is a picture of 'The Arms of Governor MacQuarie', which has every appearance of the MacQuarrie of MacQuarrie's coat of arms.

After his father's death Lachlan with his mother and the rest of the family lived in Oskamull but he came under the tutelage of his uncle, Murdoch Maclaine of Lochbuie, and as a young lad joined the army. He had a long and distinguished military career, attaining the rank of major general in 1813. He saw service in Nova Scotia, Jamaica, Egypt, Ceylon and India and in 1809 he was appointed Governor General of New South Wales. During his governship the city of Sydney was laid out and what had been, on his appointment, a penal settlement, had developed into a thriving colony, later attracting settlers from Ulva and Gometra and other parts of Scotland whose descendants today hold his name in high esteem as 'the Father of Australia'.

On returning from Australia in 1821 he bought an estate in Mull which he named Jarvisfield in honour of his first wife, Jane Jarvis, who died, aged twenty-three, when he was serving in India. His second wife, whom he married in 1807, was Elizabeth Henrietta Campbell, a daughter of John Campbell of Airds. Their only son, and his heir, also called Lachlan, was born in Sydney in 1814.

Major General MacQuarie intended building a mansion house more fitting for a person of his standing than the small cottage he first occupied at Gruline. It was in his time the pleasant village of Salen was laid out and he had ambitious plans to develop it as a fishery village and to set up a distillery there. It was he as heritor who applied to the Commissioners for Building Churches in the Highlands to have Salen included in their list of Parliamentary charges. He died, however, in London in 1824, four years before the manse was built and the ruinous church there was repaired and enlarged.

Lachlan, his son, was fourteen years old when the buildings were completed and it was on his behalf that the land was conveyed by James Drummond (sixth Viscount Strathallan) 'Tutor Dative of Lachlan MacQuarie, only son of the deceased Major General Lachlan MacQuarie of Jarvisfield, in the Island of Mull, late Governor of New South Wales' (Allan Maclean, *Telford's Highland Churches*).

Governor MacQuarie was buried on his estate at Gruline and sometime later a granite tomb was prepared to receive his remains and those of his wife, Elizabeth, his son, Lachlan, who died without issue, and his little daughter. (Rodney L. McQuary, *A Book about MacQuarries*.) The mausoleum at Gruline, bearing the MacQuarrie coat of arms, is maintained by the National Trust for Scotland on behalf of the owners, the National Trust for Australia (N.S.W.).

The name Jarvisfield is now retained only as the name of a road in Salen. The estate which eventually included Gruline, Salen, Pennygowan and Killiechronan right down to the Sound of Ulva was renamed Glenforsa and passed to William Drummond, the seventh Viscount Strathallan, and from him to his son-in-law, Col. Greenhill Gardyne.

America, too, offered opportunities to those islanders who could see no future for themselves and their families in the old country. What Dr John Walker described as 'the pernicious emigration to Ireland' from Mull was but the first stage of the exodus to the New World. The North American colonies, from Nova Scotia to Georgia, were crying out for colonists to develop them. Emigration societies were formed to facilitate the transfer of hopefuls from the run-down estates of home to 'the Land of Promise' ('Fearann a' Gheallaidh') overseas.

The societies sent out glowing descriptions of the opportunities that awaited those that availed themselves of the facilities offered to them. The reality did not always match the promise and accounts of what it was really like began to percolate back to the friends back home, often in the form of Gaelic songs composed by the exiles. A classic example of this genre is the poem, 'A' Choille Ghruamach' ('The Surly Forest') by John Maclean, Tiree, who emigrated to Nova Scotia in 1815.

After the War of American Independence (1775–83), it was Canada that became the main destination of trans-Atlantic migrations from the Highlands and Islands. In his account of the parish of Kilninian in the *Old Statistical Account (1792–93)* the Rev. Archibald McArthur states, 'there is no emigration to America from this parish.'

The emigrants from the Highlands and Islands took with them to their new homes the language, culture, songs, music and religion, Presbyterian or Catholic, of their place of origin, often naming their farms and townships after the places they had left behind them in the old country. Many of their descendants, living today, maintain the cultural traditions of their forebears.

From the lone shieling of the misty island,
    Mountains divide us, and the waste of seas;
Yet still the blood is strong, the heart is Highland,
    And we, in dreams, behold the Hebrides.

23

6

Migrations to the Lowlands

THE DRIFT FROM THE islands was not always overseas to the colonies. The men of Ulva had traditionally migrated south for the Lowland harvests. In the late eighteenth and early nineteenth centuries they were increasingly drawn to the industrial centres of the Lowlands where the Industrial Revolution was happening. James McAnna whose great great grandfather was born in Ulva published a pamphlet, *The Ulva Families of Shotts*, 1991, in which he gives a fascinating account of his Ulva forebears and their descendants who settled in the Lanarkshire industrial village. Many other towns and villages in the industrial belt of Scotland must have had similar communities of islanders who settled in them.

Finding Livingstone's Cave

One summer's day, on one of our explorations of Ulva, Angus and I came across a cluster of ruined houses surrounded by the green patches of ground that had once been cultivated. Some distance higher up we discovered the entrance of a cave in the basaltic rocks. Going in from the bright warm sunshine into the cold darkness of the interior was to enter into another, somewhat sinister, world. The coldness, darkness and vastness were not diminished in our telling of our discovery when we returned home. We were told that we had seen tobhta Livingstone and Livingstone's Cave.

We were told that the man who lived there was Neil Livingstone, Niall Mór, who after the battle of Culodden came to Mull. He moved to Ulva and while his house was a-building, he and his wife, Mary Morison, and their livestock lived in the cave. He later worked a small-holding at Fearann Ard Àirigh (Land of the High Shieling) and raised a family of four sons and three daughters. In 1792 he decided that the small holding could not support his growing family and he made up his mind to follow the trend of his fellow islanders and seek his livelihood in the industrial south. He settled in Blantyre, Lanarkshire and took up employment in the cotton spinning factories there.

One of his sons who was born in Ulva, Niall Beag ('Little Neil' or 'Neil Junior') married a local Blantyre woman, Agnes Hunter, and their second son, David, born in 1813, became the famous missionary explorer of Africa, Dr David Livingstone. Highlanders, ever fond of encapsulating the virtues of their heroes in pithy hyperbole described him as 'One of Scotland's greatest sons', 'One of the moral giants of our race', 'The greatest missionary since St Paul'.

David Livingstone visited Ulva in 1864. 'The minister, Mr Fraser,' he wrote, 'made inquiries some years ago and found an old woman who remembered my grandfather living at Uamh or Cave. The walls of the house remain and the corn and potato patches are green, but no-one lives there.'

The oldest document preserved in the David Livingstone Museum at Blantyre is the certificate of character given to his grandfather, Niall Mór, by the parish minister of Kilninian:

> The bearer, Neil Livingstone, a married man in Ulva, part of the parish of Kilninian, has always maintained an unblemished moral character, and is known for a man of piety and religion; he has a family of four sons, the youngest of which is three years, and three daughters, the youngest of which is six years of age. As he proposes to offer his services at some of the spinning manufactories, he and his wife, Mary Morison, and their family of children are hereby earnestly recommended for suitable engagement. Given at Ulva, this eighth January 1792 Arch. McArthur, Minister Lauchn Maclean, Elder; R. Stewart, J.P.

The late Alastair Cameron, the distinguished antiquarian who wrote under the nom de plume, 'North Argyll', contributed articles about the Livingstone family to the *Oban Times* (14/3/63 and 5/9/63). The following are two stories about Niall Mór related by Cameron in the articles:

> Around 1790 a new factor came on the estate (Colin MacDonald was the proprietor of Ulva at that time) and he proved to be a hard man. A covetous neighbour set his eyes on acquiring the croft of Neil Mór and he went to the factor with a trumped-up story of accusation which the factor believed, and he immediately served Niall Mór with a notice of

eviction at the next term. However, before this arrived, the falsity of the accusation had been proved to the factor. He lost no time interviewing Livingstone and told him he need not go. But his reply to this was that he could not remain under a man who believed a defamatory story against him without hearing his side. 'I am ready to go,' he said, 'and go I will.'

The other story about Niall Mór related by Alastair Cameron describes the death bed scene of the old man in Blantyre:

When the old man was on his death bed in Blantyre, he gathered his family together and told them that, going back six generations of Livingstones, he had not discovered a dishonest man among them; therefore if any of them or their descendants proved otherwise it would not be because it was in their blood. He ended by leaving them the precept, 'Be honest.'

Some years ago, in conversation with Dr Hubert F. Wilson, a grandson of David Livingstone, I told him about finding Livingstone's cave when I was a boy in Ulva, and repeated what I had heard about the death-bed scene. Dr Wilson was interested, and he told me that he had never been to Ulva but that the story of his great great grandfather's last words remained in the family tradition.

David Livingstone died on 1st May, 1873 and he was buried with National Honours in Westminster Abbey on 18th April, 1874.

Wars, emigration overseas and migration to the Lowlands were contributary factors in the decline in the population of Ulva but by the turn of the century two other factors were emerging which were to result in the remarkable turnaround in population, from 266 in 1764 to 604 in 1837. The manufacture of kelp and the cultivation of potatoes were the two new factors in the equation that were to bring about the dramatic change.

7

Kelp and Potatoes

AFTER THREE YEARS, CAPTAIN Dugald Campbell, the first of the 'New Men', sold Ulva to Colonel Charles Campbell of Barbreck who, in turn, sold it in 1785 to Colin MacDonald of Boisdale. On Colin's death in 1800 he was succeeded by his son Ranald who remained proprietor until 1821. The thirty-six years of the MacDonald ownership saw the remarkable rise in Ulva's population and in the prosperity, short-lived in the event, of the lairds and their tenants.

Colin MacDonald was the son of Alasdair MacDonald of Boisdale, a brother of the chief of Clan Ranald. It was this Alasdair who in 1745 met Prince Charles Edward on board the Du Teillay and advised him to abandon his campaign. 'Go home' he bluntly advised the Prince who replied with dignity, 'I have come home.' This Alasdair was known in the Outer Isles as Alasdair Mór nam Mart ('Big Alasdair of the Cattle') on account of his successful dealings as a drover. He is also credited with having introduced kelp manufacture from Ireland to the

Hebrides in 1735 and, eight years later, also from Ireland, the cultivation of potatoes. It is said that he instructed his tenants in Uist to cultivate potatoes extensively much against the inclination of the people who are reputed to have said that he could force them to plant the despised tubers but he could not force them to eat them! (John L. Campbell, *Songs Remembered in Exile.*) By 1780 potatoes had become the staple food of all the Hebrides, replacing the oatmeal that had been so long the Highlanders' preference.

The MacDonald lairds of Ulva inherited the entrepreneurial spirit of their ancestor and exploited to the full the opportunities offered by their situation and times. The development of machinery and the rapid growth of the factory system that characterised the Industrial Revolution of the late eighteenth and early nineteenth centuries created a demand for raw materials. The demand for the soda ash that was used in the production of soap, glass and linen was previously supplied by barilla imported from France and Spain, but during the wars of this period, when the supply of barilla was either cut off or subjected to heavy import duties, the demand had to be met from home-grown sources.

Growing naturally in great abundance round the shores of the Western Isles were the seaweeds suitable for kelp-making. The seaweeds round the rocky coasts of Ulva 'produced the best kelp in the Western Isles, fetching the highest price in the market' (*New Statistical Account*), and entered into the voluminous corpus of traditional Gaelic proverbs:

Barr òir a' cuartachadh Eilean Ulbhaidh
(A golden crop surrounds the Isle of Ulva – (*The Campbell Collection of Gaelic Proverbs*, ed. Donald E. Meek)

In the early years of the kelp industry the profits were modest, but during the boom years around the turn of the century some island proprietors made enormous profits out of a marine plant that cost them nothing to produce and that could be harvested and processed by their tenants for a very modest outlay. Another bonus that accrued to the landlord from the kelp industry was that his tenants could pay their rents to him from the cash they earned from kelping. Whole families could find gainful employment during the summer months. The younger women cut the seaware from the rocks with sickles; older women and children could carry the wet weeds to the drying and burning pits in creels; men, young and old, supervised the gathering, drying and burning processes. It is reckoned that twenty tons of wet seaweed produced one ton of kelp. A kelping team made up from one family, perhaps, could earn eight pounds for a season's labour.

The island proprietors who had previously encouraged, sometimes forcibly, the emigration of their tenants now took measures to ensure that their estates had the large populations that were required to manufacture the kelp, but the holdings in Ulva were too small to sustain the expanding population. Oatmeal had long been the staple food of the islanders but oats and barley required well cultivated arable land and by the middle of the eighteenth century large quantities of oatmeal had to be imported from the mainland to Mull. The cultivation of potatoes was the answer to the problem. In 1764 Dr John Walker was writing 'The greatest improvement ever made in the island (Mull) has been of late years by the planting of potatoes. Was their cultivation confined to waste ground it would be a regulation of great advantage both to the proprietors and tenants as the bulk of the reclaimable land is precisely adapted for being subdued and brought into culture by potatoes.' (John Walker's *Report on the Hebrides*, ed. Margaret M. McKay). Potatoes could be grown on poor soil, took up less ground than cereals to provide a year's supply for a family and provided most of the nutrients necessary to sustain life. In short, potato cultivation enabled large populations to exist, or at least subsist on small lots. The larger the population, the more kelp produced, the more kelp produced, the greater the proprietors' profits.

Colin MacDonald had the reputation of being a progressive and considerate landlord. Ulva House was built in his time and extensions were added later by his son. When he died in 1800 he was 'deeply lamented'. His second wife, the daughter of Captain Robert Campbell of Glen Falloch, after his death continued the caring concern towards the tenants shown by him. Ranald, Colin's eldest son by his second wife, commonly known as Staffa MacDonald or simply Staffa, became sole proprietor of Ulva on the death of his father, and he, too, was very attentive to the well-being of the islanders and was, in turn, revered by them. In his time the estate was enlarged by the acquisition of Little Colonsay, Inch Kenneth, Gometra and part of Gribun. Many improvements in methods of cultivation, notably the enclosure of fields and reseeding of grass lands were carried out by him and it was he who introduced the Cheviot breed of sheep to the island. His tenants lived in very comfortable circumstances, each tenant having at least two cows, a kailyard and a boat. Their diet included the fish that were so plentiful round the coasts and home-produced beef and mutton. He sent a young man from Ulva South to learn the baker's trade which he practised on his return home. Other shops were opened in the island at this time.

Staffa MacDonald was active in the promotion of education in the islands and in the preservation of the Gaelic culture of his people. He played the part of a Highland chief of earlier times complete with a personal piper, sharing with his friend, Sir Walter Scott, romantic notions of the past. He had a large circle of friends who were attracted to him by his personal charm and many of them were lavishly entertained by him in Ulva House. Sir Walter Scott visited Ulva twice during his time and expressed his admiration of the Chief of Ulva's Isle. In a letter to a friend Sir Walter used a phrase which sums up Ranald's highest achievement as laird of Ulva: 'He trebled his income and doubled his population by attention to his kelp shores.' (The foregoing two paragraphs are based on information given by R.W. Munro and Alan Macquarrie in *Clan MacQuarrie – A History*.)

In 1812 Ranald married Elizabeth Margaret Steuart, only daughter and heiress of Henry (later Sir Henry) Steuart of Allanton, LLB, a member of a family of long pedigree. He carried out experiments in arboriculture, pioneering the system of transplanting large trees which was described in 1827 in his greatly acclaimed *Planter's Guide* (James McAnna, *The Ulva Families of Shotts*.)

Ranald's highest achievement as summed up by Sir Walter Scott contained the seeds that were to produce serious problems in the future for subsequent owners who, when the kelp boom was over, were faced with over-populated estates with no alternative industry available on which to base a stable economy. By 1815 the price of kelp had fallen so low that its manufacture was becoming unprofitable, and Ranald was finding himself in serious financial difficulties. By 1816 he had 'granted a trust disposition in favour of his creditors which conveyed his estates into the hands of trustees who were given possession in 1817' (*Clan MacQuarrie – A History*). Parts of the estate were sold and in 1821 Ulva itself was bought by Ranald's father-in-law, Sir Henry Steuart, Bt, of Allanton.

Ranald was represented in the protracted negotiations by his friend the lawyer John Forman and retained the title 'of Staffa' to the end of his life. Ranald's relationship with his father-in-law deteriorated at this time, but he succeeded to the baronetcy and to the estate of Allanton on the death of Sir Henry. When Ranald's wife succeeded her mother as the heiress of the Setons of Touch he assumed the grandiose style of Sir Ranald (or Reginald) MacDonald Steuart-Seton (or Seton-Steuart) of Staffa, Allanton and Touch, Bt. He was the sheriff of Stirlingshire until he died in 1838.

The new owner of Ulva, Sir Henry Steuart, Bt, of Allanton, had no plans for retaining it in the family for more than a limited period and there is no evidence that he spent much, or any, time on the island. His name did not occur in local island traditions. We were led to believe that Ranald MacDonald had sold out to two brothers, Alexander and John Forman, sons of a baker in Stirling. I can only conclude that they were members of the trustees into whose hands Ranald had granted a trust disposition in favour of his creditors and who were given possession of Ulva in 1817, and that in the protracted negotiations between 1817 and 1821 when Sir Henry finally took possession, the names of the trustees would be prominent in the correspondence. The name John Forman appears as Ranald's friend and lawyer.

Sir Henry either personally or through his factor in Ulva actively engaged in efforts to improve his island estate during his brief time as proprietor and a very full, if perhaps over-optimistic, account is found among the

Ulva Estate Papers, 'particulars of the Estate of Ulva, Argyleshire. Advertised for Sale' with a detailed 'Rental of Ulva for the Year 1824'. The following details are taken from these papers.

The proprietor (he is not named in the papers) made commendable efforts to improve the estate. 'Capital', says the report, 'as well as the example of a spirited landlord is requisite to give energy to such undertaking.' There is evidence that the landlord of Ulva during those four years provided both. The first two years, 1821 and 1822, were 'the worst that this country ever saw for the sale of all produce' but the Ulva kelp 'uniformly bore a large price and was sought after with eagerness by the dealers'. The kelp revenue for Ulva in 1824 was £600 (100 tons at £6 per ton). The kelp shores had been extended by judicious planting of the vacant shores, 'whereby the proprietor within the last three years had added about 25 tons of kelp, or £150 to the yearly rental for the small outlay of £160.'

Shell-marle from the shores, spread as a fertiliser on the fields, greatly increased the production of potato and turnip crops and of grass and hay. The 'spirited' proprietor also gave a lead in developing the fishing potential of the coastal waters. He fitted out a small open boat with four men aboard who in a few weeks 'with little dexterity or science' caught two tons of cod and ling of superior quality, worth £20 per ton on the Glasgow market. The report goes on: 'The oysters of Ulva are still more celebrated . . . were the fishing of oysters put on a proper footing, it would be adequate to the supply of the City of Glasgow, with a better article than it has at present . . . the proprietor has already done something towards spreading the knowledge of a scientific mode of fishing by providing oyster dredgers of the best construction. A small boat with only two men, last year, made an attempt to exercise their skill, and in two days, they loaded it with fine oysters which they sold at Tobermory, and other parts of the Mull coast, for £12 sterling.'

The population of Ulva in 1824 is given as 600, living in 18 townships. Seventy-two tenant farmers paid a total rent of £1142 11/6. The upset price was £37,860 19/6, calculated on the basis of twenty-seven years of land rent and fourteen years' kelp revenue. 'The inhabitants are a frugal and industrious race . . . the smaller tenants live chiefly by the rearing of cattle, on lots of land leased out to them, by fishing and by the making of kelp. By the occupation last mentioned many of them make a very handsome profit, besides paying their rent.'

The Ulva estate, 'probably the most compact and beautiful Highland property now on the market', including 'the beautiful Farm of Laggan, esteemed the most desirable in Mull' was bought in 1895 by Lt. Col. Charles MacQuarie of Glenforsa, a younger brother of Maj. Gen. Lachlan MacQuarie, Governor General of New South Wales. Once again Ulva belonged to a member of a clan that had been associated with it for hundreds of years. No doubt his return to the land of his forebears raised the hopes of the islanders, not least those of the one hundred and fifty of them who, according to Jo Currie, bore the name MacQuarrie. One of his first actions on taking possession of his new estate was to ensure that the islanders were provided with a church, with a manse and glebe for a minister. It was an act of faith on his part and on the part of the Commissioners for Building Churches, demonstrating their confidence in the island's future development. As time went by, however, it became more and more evident that that confidence could not be sustained, and emigration was being seen as a solution to the problem of over-population.

How Charles MacQuarie would have responded to the problem which he had acquired and obviously did not envisage may never be known. He died in Ulva in 1835 and was buried in the old ancestral burial ground at Kilvickewan.

8

The Clarks of Ulva 1835–1935

THE PROPRIETOR OF ULVA in our time was Francis William Clark III. His son was the fourth in direct descent to bear that name, and as the heir is often referred to as the 'young laird' it is not surprising that there has been some misunderstanding as to how many of the four Francis William Clarks, were actually lairds of Ulva. There were, in fact, only two – the first and his grandson, the laird of our time. For almost exactly a hundred years, from November 1835 when the first Francis William bought Ulva, to October 1935 when the third Francis William died, Ulva belonged to those two Clarks.

The trustees of Lt. Col. Charles MacQuarie sold Ulva to Francis William Clark I, a sheriff in Stirling, for £29,500, with entry at Martinmas 1835. He was born in Elgin in 1800 and he died in Ulva, where he is buried, in 1887, his son, Francis William II, having predeceased him.

One of the most remarkable and informative contributions to the *New Statistical Account* for Argyll is his description of the parishes of Kilninian, Kilmore and Ulva. The name of the parish minister of Kilninian and Kilmore, Rev. D. McArthur D.D. appears in the heading of the report, but a footnote is added at the foot of the page, 'Drawn up by Francis William Clark, Esq. of Ulva. September 1843.'

It tells us much about the man himself, his hopes and plans, his enthusiasms and good intentions, his commitment to improvement and to the welfare of his tenants. It is difficult to identify the Clark of this report with the Clark of the ruthless evictions that were to follow a few years after its publication.

Two years after he bought Ulva he prepared a detailed and accurate census of the parish:

District	No. of Families	No. of people
Ulva	116	604
Gometra	26	168
Mull mainland	40	222
Colonsay	1	6
Totals	183	1000

Part of the report reads like a pastoral idyll with scenes of happy and contented inhabitants at the summer shielings, celebrating with piping, dancing and feasting, the young women spinning and preparing the dairy produce. The laird, who had learned Gaelic, delighted in the old tales told by the people. They were healthy, peaceably disposed and religiously inclined, not over-industrious, perhaps, but abstemious, their only vices, apparently, being their indulgence in snuff, tobacco and – among women – tea.

The superior soil and climate produced good crops. A

sample of the first wheat ever grown in the Hebrides was sent to the Highland Society's Agricultural Museum, as were also three potatoes, each weighing two pounds, grown in the Home Farm which also produced 900 barrels of potatoes. Considerable quantities of potatoes were also grown by the tenants and exported and the Scots barley (bear) which they grew could be sold to the Tobermory distillery. Black cattle and horses were reared and also exported and 100 tons of kelp, the best in the Western Isles, fetching the highest price in the market was manufactured annually.

The farms were divided and enclosed. Near the shore was the arable land; more inland the pastures and, beyond that again, separated by a stone dyke running round the island, the sheep walk or hill ground where the tenants' sheep and horses are grazed. The proprietor introduced longer-term leases and encouraged the tenants to improve the soil by tillage, clearing of stones and laying lime shell sand.

Fish and shellfish of every description abounded round the shores, and Ulva, with its good harbours, could become a fishing station for cod, ling and herring. Every tenant had a boat, some more than one.

The community was served by a full range of tradesmen – shoemakers, square-wrights, boat carpenters, tailors, weavers, blacksmiths, dry-stone masons, merchants, all, more or less, engaged in agriculture. The post office on the island dealt with 2,600 letters, received and dispatched, and 340 newspapers annually.

The growing tourist trade was catered for. The old inn at the pier was repaired and a new innkeeper was installed, offering every accommodation to parties on pleasure trips to Staffa and men were in readiness at all times to convey them.

There were two schools in Ulva, a parochial school

and a 'charity school' run by the SSPCK. There was also a school in Gometra and, on the Mull side of the ferry, a new school was being built. The laird's mansion house is described as a large modern building, placed in an extensive park, with a garden well stocked with every kind of fruit. The Ulva church and manse, erected in 1827, 'are two neat and fine looking buildings about five minutes walk from the laird's house.'

The first minister of the new church was the Rev. Neil Maclean, who was presented to the Parliamentary Charge by King George IV, and admitted on 26th August, 1828. Like many ministers of his time he combined his clerical duties with farming. He lost no time preparing his glebe for cultivation and expended seventeen pounds of his own money in blasting the outcrop of rocks on it – a substantial proportion of his annual stipend of £120. His name appears on the Rent Roll of 1841 as one of the seventy-six tenants who were paying a total yearly rent of £1173 16/-, together with a total of 236 hens, 236 dozen eggs and 502 days' service, these obligations being valued in cash: 1/- per hen, 4d per dozen eggs and 1/2 per day's labour. He farmed the Ardellum lands and paid an annual rent of thirty-three pounds but was exempt from the obligations of poultry, eggs and labour.

When the Rev. Neil Maclean was translated to Halkirk on 6th February, 1844, he was succeeded by the Rev. William Fraser, a native of Inverness, who was ordained and inducted to Ulva on 26th September the same year. He remained there until he died, unmarried, on 8th May 1874. His grave in the old churchyard of Kilninian is marked by a stone, inscribed:

Rev. William Fraser, A.M.
Minister of Ulva
died 1874
62 years of age
30 years of his ministry
Erected by a cousin.

Nearby is another headstone: Christina Munro, died 1856, aged 82. Erected by her son, Wm Fraser, Minister of Ulva.

If Neil Maclean's sixteen-year ministry coincided with the golden age of Clark's account, William Fraser's thirty years ministry covered the darkest and most terrible times in the history of the people of Ulva.

9

The Year the Potato Departed, and the Evictions that Followed

ALTHOUGH FRANCIS WILLIAM CLARK I was writing in 1843 that the Ulva shores were yielding annually 100 tons of the best kelp in the Western Isles that was fetching the highest price in the market, the kelp industry which had been the mainstay of the island economy was doomed. He continued for a time operating at a loss until eventually the market for kelp had gone. And when he speaks of his tenants exporting surplus potatoes, there had already been warnings in the '30s that this crop was subject to disease – potato blight. When the potato crop in Ulva failed in 1846, 'the year the potato departed' ('A' bhliadhna a dh'fhalbh am buntàta'), the large population that was necessary to produce the kelp and who relied on potatoes for their existence were faced with destitution and starvation, with no money to pay their rents and no alternative crop with which to feed themselves and their families.

Correspondence relating to measures for the relief of distress in Scotland, July 1846, describes the plight of the people of Mull in the year the potato crop failed: 'In Mull, 8000 of the population of 10,000 subsisted as much on potatoes as did, contemporarily, the lowest class in Ireland. The crop failed in 1836, but blight years ten years later brought unprecedented want to the Highlands and Islands. Cottars subsisted on shellfish, dulse and other seaweed.' (MacLean and Carrel, *As an Fhearann.*)

Various bodies were set up to ameliorate the plight of the people and a central board to co-ordinate the efforts was established in Edinburgh with a branch in Glasgow. Prominent among the members of the Glasgow branch was the minister of St Columba's Gaelic church, the Rev. Dr Norman MacLeod, a member of the dynasty of the MacLeods of Morvern ministers to which Dr George MacLeod, Lord MacLeod of Fuinary, founder of the Iona Community, belonged. (He was the great grandson of Dr Norman.) Dr Norman MacLeod worked incessantly to relieve the sufferings of his fellow Highlanders, touring the islands, bringing their plight to the notice of the public, collecting thousands of pounds and quantities of meal for their relief. His work in organising relief in the '30s and '40s earned him the sobriquet 'Caraid nan Gaidheal' ('Friend of the Gaels') and a collection of his Gaelic prose writing was published under this title. In one of his essays in it he describes the harrowing scenes he witnessed in Tobermory where emigrants for North America were boarding 'the Big Ship of the Exiles' ('Long Mhór nan Eilthireach') leaving behind them relations and friends and their ancestral lands never to return.

One of the parish ministers who promptly responded to Dr MacLeod's request for information about the local conditions in their parishes during the 1846 potato famine was the Rev. William Fraser, minister of Ulva since 1844. He reported that the state of most of his parishioners was 'miserable beyond description'. The old hand querns were being put to use to grind what corn remained. 'I believe', he wrote, 'that it is beyond the power of many individuals to keep themselves in life till summer.' (He was writing on 31st December). 'It is a common case for me to have an application from a family of six persons, and who did not taste food, as they say, for two days previous, either for the loan of money or what will serve a diet . . . In short, I give you it as my candid opinion, that there will be many deaths here soon unless something be done here immediately.'

Prompt action was taken that averted the occurrence of the tragedy predicted by William Fraser but in the long term the collapse of the kelp industry and the potato famine made the evictions and emigrations inevitable. On one of our explorations of Ulva, Angus and I discovered the ruins of a terrace of houses just above the high-water mark on the shore of Soraby Bay at Ard Glas. 'You have been at Starvation Terrace,' they told us when we returned home. 'That is where the old and feeble folk cleared from their crofts were placed by Clark, to exist as best they could on shellfish and seaweeds till they died.' I am not sure that this simplistic explanation of the ruins we saw was the whole truth. Clark had earlier written about the suitability of Ulva for development of fishing stations, and it is possible that the terrace was a belated and futile attempt on his part to encourage people to look to the sea and seashore for their livelihood. Other evicting landlords were removing their tenants from the more fertile inland lands to the rocky, barren coastal strips in the forlorn expectation that they could earn their living as fishermen. Whatever Clark's intention might have been, 'Starvation Terrace' was aptly named and the name remains to this day.

Whatever hopes Clark may have entertained when he

bought Ulva in 1835, or whatever improvements he may have instigated or planned, the collapse of the kelp industry and the failure of the potato crop, which were due to circumstances outwith his control, compelled him to reconsider his position and decide on his course of action. He left on record a chillingly clinical analysis of the problems he faced and how he solved them in the statement made by him at Ulva on Thursday, 13th February 1851, written down by Sir John MacNeill (of the Colonsay MacNeills) and entered in the minutes of evidence of the Board of Supervision of the West Highlands and Islands (R.W. Munro and Alan *Macquarrie, Clan MacQuarrie – A History*):

When I purchased this property, kelp was manufactured upon it, about 100 tons annually, which was considered in the market as of the very best quality . . . After the reduction of the duty on barilla, and when the kelp ceased to be profitable, I continued to manufacture it at an annual loss, till within the last four years, when, finding it unsaleable, I discontinued the manufacture. At that very time came the potato failure, in consequence of which the crofters were barely able to maintain themselves, and quite unable to pay any rent . . . I have been increasing my sheep stock, as the removal of the crofters afforded space . . . Had the crofters not been removed, no rent could have been realised – the whole produce of the property would not have sufficed for their support. In the first years of the failure of the potato, I purchased meal largely from the Government stores, and elsewhere. I borrowed money under the drainage act, to the amount of £500, and have also expended more than £500 in draining and other improvements, from my own private funds, chiefly with a view to give employment to the population; but finding that the crofters could not pay their rents, and that my private resources were therefore diminished from year to year, I had no alternative but either surrender my property to the people or resume the natural possession of the land. I therefore, very reluctantly, resolved to promote the removal of the crofters, and proceeded to warn off a certain number yearly for the last four years until now. The population, which was originally about 500, is reduced to 150. This diminution has been accomplished in five years.

Some of the crofters got crofts on other properties, some of the cottars settled in Tobermory, all the others went to America, Australia or to the south of Scotland.

As the process of eviction was resolutely prosecuted during the four years 1847 to 1851 – there were eighty-eight Summons of Removal and Sequestration during that period. Clark's attitude towards the crofters hardened and became embittered. The 'peaceably disposed and religiously inclined' people of Ulva whose only vices were 'indulgence in snuff, tobacco and tea' were now considered to be 'very refractory and lawless people', 'truculent tenants who laugh to scorn the sheriff's warrant; saying they will remain where they are, independent of sheriff or me.' (T.M. Devine, *The Great Highland Famine*.) Clark, the lawyer who 'was educated to habits of business' was mortified by this stubborn show of resistance to his plans.

The diminution of the population continued for many years after 1851; by 1881 there were only fifty-three people living on Ulva. A group of crofters on the

Glenforsa estate met in the temperance hall in Salen to discuss what evidence they would submit to the Napier Commission which was due to meet in the Temperance Hall, Tobermory, on 10th August 1883. One of those present was Lachlan MacQuarrie, aged sixty-four, then living in Salen. He said that there were at that time only the proprietor (Clark) and his three shepherds, besides two or three cottars, living in Ulva. He himself had to move from a large croft at Ormaig to make way for someone who offered to pay more rent and take a smaller croft at Cragaig. Evicted from there, he had taken the couples of his house and built a hut on the shore close to the high-water mark. On seeing this the proprietor gave him a house at three pounds a year at Caolas, where he lived with his wife and three children, making a livelihood catching lobsters. He left Ulva of his own accord. 'Yes,' he reported to the commission, 'I remember when Ulva belonged to the MacQuarries [i.e. Charles MacQuarie, 1825–1835]. People were comfortable then. It is a pretty fertile island for raising oats and potatoes, but there is no crop at all now, except what the laird grows himself.' (A.D. Cameron, *Go Listen to the Crofters*.)

10

How the Evicted People of Ulva Fared in Exile

WHILE IT IS POSSIBLE to set down briefly an outline of the events that followed the collapse of the kelp industry and the failure of the potato crop by quoting Clark's own analysis of the situation and his response to it, the full weight of the human misery and suffering involved can never be measured, only hinted at by reference to individual incidents and personal tragedies recorded in records made at the time or retained in the oral traditions of the evicted families and their descendants.

There are descriptions of the long voyages on the ships on which emigrants from Ulva and elsewhere were given passage overseas, assisted by the Highlands and Islands Emigration Society, ships like the *British Queen*, the *British King*, *Araminta*, *Marmion*, *Priscilla* and *Hercules*. There were tales of the gross overcrowding and the insanitary conditions in some of these ships; outbreaks of typhus, smallpox, measles and other diseases; deaths of infants and adults and burials at sea in shark-infested waters; storms at sea and shortages of food and water. And always, the sense of up-rootedness from the land of their forebears, separation from relations and friends and apprehension about their future in foreign lands hundreds of miles from the old home.

The *British Queen* sailed from Liverpool on 8th January 1852, bound for Victoria. Among the list of emigrants aboard was one who had previously embarked at Tobermory, Dugald McFarlane, aged forty. Accompanying him, were his wife, Effie (thirty-five) and their seven children, aged from fourteen years to eight months. In the column headed 'Remarks' there were the following hand-written notes:

> Has been a crofter. Was dispossessed of his land ten months ago by Clarke [sic] of Ulva. Has supported his family by catching lobsters and other shellfish. Price of lobsters 2/- per doz. Has not earned 20/- for the last month. Inhabits one room, for which he pays 7d per week. Very destitute family. The Revd Mr Ross states that he found McFarlane and two of his children lying in the bed in a state of exhaustion for want of food. Landed from *Hercules* with fever.

Dugald McFarlane, however, may have considered himself lucky, having prospects of a new life in Australia, compared with his fellow islanders who had no hope of escaping from the hunger and destitution of a life in Tobermory. Robert Somers who visited the Highlands and Islands in 1848 published, first in the *North British Daily Mail*, and later, in book form, his *Letters from the Highlands on the Famine of 1846*. In one of the letters he describes conditions in Tobermory which he witnessed at first-hand:

The result of these evictions, in a general point of view, are injurious in the extreme. They accumulate poverty and destitution in heaps. Instead of the poor being spread over their respective parishes, they are thrown together in villages, where there is no property, no agency, no resources adequate to cope with their necessities, and where, upon any unusual pressure, there is nothing but the most appalling and unmanageable destitution. The population of Tobermory has increased, in a short time, from a few families to 1000 souls; and this increase has probably resulted more from the influx of ejected paupers and cottars from the outlying parts of the island than from the wholesome influence of prosperity.

In one house he visited in Tobermory he saw a family with ten children living in one room. 'The mother,' he wrote, 'a woman of very respectable appearance, was making thin porridge for their supper. They had got a similar meal in the morning and this was their whole diet. The children were very ragged, almost naked, and on this account could not go to the Gaelic School, though admission had been offered free of charge. The room was very bare of furniture, containing only a few things which they had carried over the mountains.'

Somers paints an equally dismal picture of the exiles from the islands in the Lowland towns and cities.

Anyone who witnessed the wretched creatures who crowded into our large towns during last summer and autumn – who knows the want and privation which there awaited them – who saw hundreds of families lying night after night on the cold damp grass of Glasgow Green, or amid the still more pestilential vapours of the wynds and lanes, and who listened to the barking coughs of the infants, as if their little bosoms were about to rend, can require no statistics to satisfy their minds of the fearful destruction of human life occasioned by the eject-ment of the peasantry from the parishes in which they were born and had lived, and the property of which should have been made responsible for their sustenance in the day of famine. This country was last year the scene of a Massacre of the Innocents, which has had no equal since the days of Herod the Infanticide.

Tobermory was not the only place in Mull where the displaced people of Ulva settled and eked out a precar-ious existence. They also settled in Salen and the Ross of Mull. It was pointed out to me that new cemeteries were opened up in Tobermory and Kilpatrick in the Ross to receive their dead and these are known to the present day as the burial grounds of the people of Ulva.

While it is true that many of the evicted families survived their uprooting and that some of them and their descendants prospered in their new homes in the Lowlands and overseas, there were many who suc-cumbed, the victims of the evictions who should never be forgotten.

11

Memories of the Ulva Clearances Live On

THE VICTIMS OF THE Ulva evictions were not forgotten. The ruined deserted townships like Starvation Terrace that I saw as a boy, were constant, silent reminders of the disastrous years of the clearances and of the man who presided over the events of these years. I remember the sense of shock I felt when, as a young boy in Ulva, I heard that a near neighbour of ours had stood on the highest point of his holding and declared in a loud voice for all to hear, 'Francis William Clark, there's a smell of your name all over Scotland!' The person thus so rudely apostrophised was not the laird of our time who bore that name, but his grandfather who had removed the people to make room for sheep.

In an era in which large-scale evictions were commonplace – those in Torloisg and Glengorm, for example – this Francis William Clark gained a notoriety that matched or exceeded that of the evicting landlords of his time. 'Notorious', 'ruthless', 'cruel', 'callous' are some of the epithets that are attached to his name.

I have before me now a cutting from an unidentified newspaper of a poem in English, entitled 'Glen Ulva', the first stanza of which reads:

'Twas on a misty summer morn
   I wandered in the glen,
By chance I saw the ruined cots
   Of a thousand Highland men;
The cruel, callous Lowland laird
   Had made them cross the deep,
And in their stead he filled the dales
   With flocks of Cheviot sheep.

The Ulva evictions had much in common with evictions elsewhere in the islands, but there were features in the Ulva saga which are distinctive and which may account for the degree of opprobrium attached to Clark's name. His estate consisted of a small island, a clearly defined territorial area, inhabited by a clearly identifiable population – na h-Ulbhaich. They were uprooted from their ancestral lands and dispersed throughout the world in an indecently short period of time – Jo Currie quotes one commentator as saying, 'He was slipping them away as fast as he could get them across the ferry' – without, apparently, any regard to their fate once they were gone.

Unlike clearances elsewhere, in the Ulva evictions there was no middle man to act as a buffer between laird and tenants; no factor (Bàillidh) to absorb the animosity of the people; no Patrick Sellars, no James Kinloch. There was no ambitious incomer who insisted that the land be cleared in order to create a larger farm for himself, like John MacColl, Kilchoan, or the Stewarts in Park, Lewis and South Harris. In his account of the clearances, Clark uses the first personal pronoun throughout – 'I had no alternative . . .', 'I resolved to promote the removal of the crofters . . .', 'I proceeded to warn off a certain number yearly . . .'

Coupled with the factor in Gaelic demonology was the minister of the established Church who was often regarded by the people as being on the side of the laird. A humorous Gaelic song reflects the popular perception of the factor and the minister as the twin oppressors of the people. In translation it goes:

The minister and the factor,
The factor and the minister.
Although the factor treated me miserably,
It was the minister that oppressed me.

The king is coming to the country,
It's my desire he should come,
To behead the factor,
And give death to the minister!

It has been suggested that the large number of Highlanders who adhered to the newly formed Free Church at the time of the Disruption in 1843 was due to this perceived attitude towards the parish ministers as being the Lairds' men. The ministers of Ulva and Kinlochspelvie did not go over to the Free Church at that time, and the Rev William Fraser who was minister of Ulva from 1844 to 1874, in his letter in response to Dr Norman MacLeod's appeal for information about conditions in Ulva at the time of the potato famine in 1846 reveals his deep concern over the dire plight of his parishioners. What he thought of the subsequent evictions is not on record.

Evidence submitted to the Napier Commission which met at Tobermory in 1883, quoted by Lorn Macintyre in his article on Ulva in the *Scots Magazine*, September 1984, reinforces the popular conception of Clark as the cruel, callous evictor. Lachlan MacQuarrie (mentioned earlier) and Alexander Fletcher testified that 'some of these evicted families were first removed from sufficient farms to smaller ones, then they were moved to a house and grass for a cow or two, then to nothing at all, and when they would not clear off altogether some of them had the roofs taken off their huts . . . In another case there was a very sick woman with her daughter in one of the houses Clark wished to have pulled down. Notwithstanding the critical condition of the woman, he had the roof taken down to a small bit over the sick woman's bed.'

Lachlan MacQuarrie further testified that near his own house there was a well. He remembered one day seeing a poor woman fetching water at it. 'When she, terrified at seeing Mr Clark coming, ran away, and left her kettle at the well, which Mr Clark took hold of and smashed to pieces.' Evidence was not given to the commission under oath nor were the witnesses immune from libel actions. Old Clark was still alive and living in Ulva when the commission met in Tobermory. He did not make any attempt to refute the evidence, nor was any action made to make him answerable for his deplorable behaviour if true. His son, Francis William II was also alive at that time, and tradition has it that he angrily remonstrated with his father over the clearances, saying that he would rather have a cailleach (an old woman) to light his pipe in every ruined house than all the sheep that roamed the sheep-walks of Ulva.

The old man, Francis William Clark, died in 1887, predeceased by his wife and his son, and was buried in the family burial ground which was enclosed by a circular wall with no entrance, which he had caused during his lifetime to be erected on Dun Bhioramuil, a small conical hillock difficult of access. A large marble cross marks his grave.

The public opprobrium attached to Clark's name continued beyond his death. I have read, but did not hear personally, two stories about the Clark burial ground and memorial stone. Howard and Jones in *The Isle of Ulva, A Visitor's Guide* recall that when the Clark memorial was being constructed, a horse-drawn wagon bearing a huge marble slab became so mired in the boggy approach that the slab had to be unloaded in order to free the vehicle. The stone lay where it had been dumped, sinking into the moss year after year until now when nobody knows exactly where it lies.

Another story, or perhaps another version of the story, related in David Craig's *On the Crofters' Trail*, tells how, when Clark's tombstone was being brought ashore at Ulvaferry, its weight and size created difficulties for those handling it. An observer summed up the situation in a succinct phrase: 'It could not be moved because of the weight of evil that was in it.'

It is not uncommon for Highlanders to imagine or invent something unchancy about the grave of a tyrant. The John MacColl, Kilchoan, mentioned earlier, was the farmer at Mingarry who persuaded Stanhope's factor to evict the crofters of four townships in order to enlarge his farm. During MacColl's lifetime, his 'elegy' was composed by Dr John MacLachlan of Rahoy. The poet prophesied that, when MacColl died, no daisy, primrose or blade of grass would grow on his grave. I remember Angie Henderson, Tobermory, whose people had Kilchoan connections, telling me that he had visited MacColl's grave and found it, indeed bare. He added: 'But if I had seen flowers growing there I would have plucked them out.'

12

The Last of the Clarks of Ulva

THE FRANCIS WILLIAM CLARK who bought Ulva in 1835 had a son, Francis William Clark, LLB, who was sheriff of Lanarkshire and who was 'widely famed for his scholarship and culture' (Angus Henderson, *The Scottish Field*). He married Catherine MacLachlan, a daughter of Dugald MacLachlan, D.L., of Killiemore (Kilfinichen) and Laudale (Morvern) and his wife Isabella. Isabella was one of the Stewarts of Achadasheanaig (later Glenaros) who figure prominently in Mull traditions as drovers and tacksmen. Two Stewart brothers, Robert and Duncan, held extensive lands from the Duke of Argyll, stretching from Glenaros on the Sound of Mull to Oskamull on Loch nan Ceall, in the eighteenth century. This could have been the R. Stewart, J.P., who appended his signature to the Certificate of Character issued to Neil Livingstone in 1792 by the Rev. Arch. McArthur, parish minister of Kilninian.

Catherine MacLachlan, who married Clark, had brothers who were 'widely known and highly respected gentlemen throughout Argyll. Mr Dugald MacLachlan, writer, banker and county clerk, Lochgilphead; Mr John MacLachlan, writer and banker, Tobermory and Mr C.H. MacLachlan, sheriff-substitute for Argyll.' (Angus Henderson.)

Sheriff Clark and his wife Catherine had a son, Francis William Clark III, the proprietor of Ulva in our time. He was educated at Glasgow University and Balliol College, Oxford, graduating BA and MA, and he was called to the Bar at the Inner Temple in 1885. The death of his father the following year put an end to what promised to be a successful career in the legal profession and when his grandfather, the first Francis William, died, aged eighty-seven in 1887, he succeeded as laird of Ulva.

In 1910 he married Caroline Sophia Hutton, elder daughter of Crompton Hutton, JP, of Harescombe Grange, Gloucestershire and their only son, the fourth Francis William, was born in 1912. Mrs Clark was a cousin of Beatrix Potter.

My recollection of the laird of Ulva was of a man, spare of frame, whose gnarled fingers and hands and drawn face suggested to me that he suffered from some form of rheumatism. He dressed in plus-two suits of a Lovat green or grey colour on account of which the estate workers called him – not to his face – 'Am Fear Liath' ('The Grey Man'). He had a reputation among them of being a fair and just employer, earning their respect if not their affection. He was a Justice of the Peace for Argyll and in 1919 he was appointed a member of the Education Authority of Argyll newly set up under the Education Act (Scot.) 1918. He was one of the two representatives from Mull; the other was Charles MacQuarrie, Ulva House, Bunessan.

I have no recollections of Mrs Clark, but I have a

memory of returning home from a Christmas party given by her and her husband in the big house to the island children when I was about three years old. I remember nothing of the party itself or of our hostess. All I remember is walking home in the cold, dark evening, clutching the paper napkin that contained brightly coloured, delicious, sticky sweeties that each child was given on leaving the house.

I have the impression that the Clarks 'kept themselves to themselves' as we say, busying themselves, he in the running of the estate, she in planning and planting the garden, but having little to do with the social life of the community. One of the few local news items in the *Oban Times* in which they feature is a report of a presentation in Ulvaferry school to Dr Reginald MacDonald, our doctor and his young bride (Dr Flora, as she became known) on the occasion of their marriage – 'a valuable marble clock' to him and a beautiful case of stainless silver cutlery' to her. 'Captain F.W. Clark presided' and spoke of Dr MacDonald's good services and how much they valued his work in this outpost of his wide district. Mrs Clark in a few words made the presentations.

Their only son was the fourth Francis William Clark. I remember seeing him from time to time, walking about the island by himself, a tall, lanky lad about five years older than myself, dressed like his father, carrying a gun, presumably to shoot rabbits. He was sent to a private boarding school, Cargilfield, and I heard that on the day before leaving, he took off on his own, with his gun, in a futile attempt to avoid his imminent banishment from the island he obviously loved. I envied him his beautiful gun and empathised with his attempt to retain his freedom. His protest was shortlived, however, and off he went the next day as planned. He continued his education at

Winchester and joined the Regular Army, obtaining a commission in the 1st Argyll and Sutherland Highlanders. He had attained the rank of Major when he was killed in action in Italy in 1944, survived by his widow and son, Francis Malcolm Clark.

Although he was sometimes referred to as the young laird of Ulva, he did not succeed his father as proprietor of Ulva. When the father died in 1935 the estate passed to his widow, and it was she who ran it during the difficult war years until she sold it in 1945 to Edith, Lady Congleton, granddaughter of Donald Smith, 1st Baron Strathcona and Mount Royal. After the sale, Mrs Clark lived in Oban and Edinburgh where she died in 1958. During her latter years she was faithfully attended by Belle Munro, the daughter of Rob Munro, the estate cattleman in our time.

During the ten years of Mrs Clark's ownership, more than half of them under wartime conditions, the estate was deteriorating. It is ironic that the first Clark of Ulva cleared the people off the land to make room for sheep; now all the sheep were being cleared but not to make room for people. When Ulva was sold 'there were only fifty-seven cattle of all classes, work horses and no sheep on the island, all the farm work, was done by horses; there was no mechanisation but one elderly tractor.' (Estate Papers.) The garden, once so lovingly cared for and cultivated, was overgrown and neglected; the buildings, including Ulva House, in a state of disrepair; the arable land under cultivation limited and the bracken had become a serious menace. Ulva, under the last of the Clarks, shared similar features with the Ulva under the last of the MacQuarries: the male heir killed in battle far from home, the land almost in a state of nature, but capable of improvement.

Nine years after Lady Congleton bought Ulva, the big house which had been the home of the Clarks for over a hundred years, was destroyed by fire during renovations and demolished. The only tangible memorials of the Clarks' century-long connections with Ulva that remained to be seen were the scores of ruined, empty houses, the enclosed family burial place on Dun Bhioramuil and a plaque on the War Memorial in the Ulva churchyard:

1939–45
IN
GRATEFUL MEMORY OF
MAJOR FRANCIS WILLIAM CLARK
OF ULVA. A & SH
MARY MELOSINE MACNEILL
WLA
WHO GAVE FAITHFUL SERVICE
IN THE GREAT WORLD WAR

13

Ulva 1918–29 – Boyhood Memories

THE TRAGIC YEARS OF the clearances lay in the past; the run-down of the estate was in a future that could not be predicted or imagined. The Ulva of my boyhood was a place of peace and contentment, where people lived in neighbourly harmony, where no child went ragged or hungry, where men and women attained old age, sound in mind and body, where there were no dole queues, no rickets, no decaying overcrowded tenements, none of the evils of 'the hungry twenties' in the cities.

No doubt my childish memories of those years are coloured by the proverbial rose-tinted spectacles, but, in later years, comparing my boyhood impressions with those of my contemporaries, I was pleased to learn that my impressions were, more or less, corroborated by theirs. I have the old family scrapbook in which my father kept cuttings from newspapers and journals of news item, and articles he had contributed over the years. He was the Ulvaferry correspondent to the *Oban Times*, and week by week the local news about people and events were reported by him. In them I find confirmation of my opinion that Ulva was a good place to live in.

Of the eleven families I remember living in Ulva, most of them lived at the east end of the island, within a mile radius of the ferry. Of the former townships around the coasts only two were inhabited – Bearnas and Cràgaig – with one family in each, the MacNeills at Bearnas in the northwest and the MacInnes at Cràgaig on the south side. We referred to the MacNeills as Neil Bearnas, Calum Bearnas, Charlie Bearnas, etc., and we knew John MacInnes of Cràgaig as 'Bodach an Taobh Deas' – 'the Old Man of the South Side'. He was, in fact, the only man then living at the once populous south side of the island. His son, John, became one of the best known and most senior of the legendary breed of MacBrayne's captains.

At Bracadale, near the big house where the laird and his wife and son lived, were the houses where the principal estate workers lived: Colin Fletcher, the manager, who succeeded John MacGillivray in 1919, with his wife, two sons and a daughter, Rob Munro and family, the cattleman, two brothers from Coll, Donald and John Kennedy who worked the horses that drew the farm implements – plough, harrow, roller, spreader, rake, reaper and ruck-lifter. After Colin Fletcher and his family left Ulva in 1930, John Kennedy succeeded him and Donald became chauffeur to the Clarks in place of Alastair Fletcher. Roderick MacNeill, who lived with his wife and a large family at Ardellum Lodge, worked on the estate, sometimes driving a cart pulled by a chestnut mare called Irene. The dairymaid, Sheila MacFadyen, and her son Sandy lived near the ferry in the only thatched house in the island.

The estate employed members of the families in seasonal tasks – potato planting, turnip hoeing, harvesting and hay-making. Rabbits were kept down by means of snares, ferrets and nets, shotguns. A pair of rabbits could be bought for eight old pence. Young men worked in the gardens and young women were employed in the big house.

The ferryman during most of our time was Angus MacGillivray who succeeded a MacPhail. He lived in the ferry house with his wife, Mary Ann, her father, 'Bodach' Cowan, her sister, Jessie and Jessie's son, Donald, who helped his uncle. In a house on Croit Phàraig a' Chaolais on the shore of Loch-a-Tuath, not far from the manse Malcolm MacDougall (Calum Dughallach) lived. We could hear him on fine summer evenings, calling his cow home for milking: 'Bó Lilidh! Bó Lilidh! Bó Lilidh!' He was a sailor, working on ocean-going ships as well as on coastal vessels. Crossing the inlet of the loch in front of his house one can still see the weirs (caraidhean) which trapped the fish when the tide receded.

The shores provided a source of income for whelk gatherers, mostly women, who picked the shellfish from the rocks at low tide and filled the sacks which were sent south to Billingsgate for sale. Some of the men caught lobsters.

The laird of Gometra in our time was Roderick Maclean (Ruadhraidh Mór Ghómastra). A native of Dervaig, he went as a young man to Glasgow and by his industry and talents made good in the retail trade so that he was able to buy the estate. He was a large, genial, Gaelic-speaking Muileach who worked alongside his employees in the hayfields and took the tiller of his own launch. He was married to Flora MacDonald, a sister of the MacDonalds who farmed Laggan, the children and grandchildren of well-known ministers of the Outer Hebrides. Most of the people of Gometra worked on the estate, but one family, the MacFarlanes, manned the brightly painted motor launches – 'the red boats' – that met the pleasure steamers off Staffa to convey the summer tourists on board to and from Fingal's Cave.

On the Mull mainland part of the parish, the farms of Oskamull, Laggan and Kilbrennan maintained families in comfortable circumstances and gave employment to local people. Mrs Naomi Campbell, a widow with four of a family, was the schoolmistress and also the postmistress. The post office was a small shed in the schoolhouse grounds. Sandy Black was the mail contractor and was the first person to have a car for hire in the parish. Hugh and Lachie MacNeill, two brothers, were successively our post men.

For the elderly, the old age pension, introduced by Lloyd George, gave a measure of security and independence, and for men who returned from the First World War with disabilities there were pensions. I remember seeing some of them, from far and near, coming to the manse to get a letter from my father in support of their claims. He was considered to be 'good with the pen' (math leis a' pheann.) Bursaries were available to enable bright boys and girls to pursue higher education in schools at Tobermory or Oban and at the colleges and universities of Glasgow and Edinburgh.

Most of the families in the parish were of Mull stock and had surnames common in Mull – MacGillivray, MacPhail, MacFadyen, MacFarlane, MacDougall, Maclean, MacDonald, Campbell. The surname Cowan in Mull was said to be derived from the cowans, dry-stane dykers, who came to Mull in the the eighteenth century. The surnames MacKenzie, MacLeod and some MacDonalds indicated incomers from the Outer Isles. Among the more unusual surnames were Cleaver and MacNeillage, which

I have never come across anywhere else.

The commonest boys' names were: Alasdair, Angus, Calum, Donald, Hugh (Eóghann), John (Iain, Seonaidh), Neil, Roderick (Ruaraidh), Colin (Cailean) and Lachie. The ten commonest names for girls were: Annie, Chrissie, Flora, Jeannie, Jessie, Joan (Seonag), Katie, Maggie, Mary and Sarah (Mór, Mórag).

There were surprisingly few nicknames. The laird was referred to by his employees as 'Am Fear Liath' on account of the colour of his suits; Duncan Campbell was 'the Duke' (simply, I think, because he was a Campbell); 'An Druid' ('the Starling'); Alan MacDonald, Dervaig, was Alan Dally because his father had business dealings with the firm Daleys of Glasgow. Calum MacDougall was called 'Dick' by his wife. People were called after farms or places they lived in, Neil MacNeill was called 'Neil Bearnas'; MacInnes who farmed Kilbrennan was 'Bodach Chill Bhrianain'; MacInnes, Cràgaig, was 'Bodach an Taobh Deas'.

The colours 'dubh' (black) and 'ruadh' (red) appended to a forename indicated the colour of hair – 'Anna Dhubh', 'Black-haired Annie'; 'Ailean Ruadh', 'Red-haired Alan'. 'Mór' (big) and 'beag' (small) sometimes indicated the size of a person: Alasdair Fletcher was 'Alasdair Mór' because he was tall and handsome; Maclean of Gometra was 'Ruaraidh Mór Ghómastra' because of his impressive appearance and standing in the community.

When two members of a family, a father and son, for example, shared the same forename, Mór indicated that one was senior, Beag that the other was junior – Niall Beag ('Neil Junior') was the son of Niall Mór ('Neil Senior'). Gaelic had no native equivalents of the English styles, Mr, Mrs, Miss; a married woman was designated as 'wife of husband's name'. The laird, Mr Clark, was known in Gaelic as An Cléireach ('the Clark'); his wife was known as 'Bean a' Chléirich'. The wife of Lachie MacNeill was not referred to as Mrs MacNeill but as 'Bean Lachie'. My mother would be known as Bean a' Mhinisteir ('the Wife of the Minister') but would be addressed in English as Mistress MacKenzie. Older married women with grown-up families, grandmothers, perhaps, were referred to as 'old ladies'. Roderick MacNeill's wife we knew as 'Cailleach Ruaraidh' ('Roderick's Old Lady'). We, as children, would be known as 'Clann a' Mhinisteir or Clann a' Mhansa' ('children of the manse').

Everyone in Ulva, young and old, spoke both Gaelic *and* English. Some were able to read and write Gaelic. Even the post's wife, Bean Lachie, who was a Londoner, had a working knowledge of Gaelic. The laird spoke Gaelic but we considered his Gaelic somewhat inelegant; his English wife was the only person, as far as I know, who did not speak Gaelic.

The Gaelic spoken in Mull at that time was pure and rich, with less intrusion of English words and phrases than that of, say, Lewis. It had an extensive vocabulary well equipped to describe objects and processes connected to island life and work, with native Gaelic words and terms to describe the fauna and flora, the weather and seasons, seedtime and harvest, landscape and seascape; to express the full range of human emotions and feelings experienced from birth to death. The conversation of the people was lit with vivid expressions and witty comments.

By the early 1920s, the Gaelic/English bilingualism of the people of Ulva had reached a state of equilibrium, with the balance, thereafter, becoming weighted in favour of English. Gaelic was the language of love and friendship; the language of hearth and home; of everyday life and work. English was the language of authority, business and officialdom, the *sine qua non* of achieving worldly success. Without English you would not 'get on' in the world. My father, who would have been described as a Gaelic enthusiast, once summed up this attitude to Gaelic in a phrase I remember over the years: 'Chan eil aran innte' ('There is now bread [i.e. livelihood] in her'). Gaelic was 'A Ghaidhlig bhog, bhlàth' ('the soft, warm Gaelic'); English was 'A' Bheurla chruaidh Shasannach' ('the hard Saxon English').

Incomers to Ulva from other islands brought with them their own dialects of Gaelic – Lewis, Uist and Coll, but this did not cause any problem in communication.

14

The Food We Ate – Shop-bought Provisions

THERE WAS NO SHOP of any kind in the parish; we depended on supplies bought from shops outwith the district. The nearest shops were at Salen, Dervaig and Tobermory. Once a week, on Saturdays, a small horse-drawn van came to Ulvaferry from Dervaig where Allan MacDonald and his sister had a shop. Allan was known throughout the island as Allan Dally, and I remember him well, a small man, neatly dressed in breeches and well-polished, brown leather leggings, perched on a plank atop of his wares and reaching under the canvas tarpaulin that covered them, producing an astonishing selection of goods while keeping up a rapid commentary commending them. What I remember best were the rosy apples, the sweet and plain biscuits, the ha'penny bars of unwrapped chocolate – Cadbury's Milk, Fry's Cream, Duncan's Hazelnut, black-striped balls, cinnamon balls and bars of toffee. Of course, he sold other commodities of a more mundane kind like tea, sugar and butter.

The people of Ulva and Gometra gathered round the

van, filling large hempen sacks with the week's supply of household groceries and swapping news. We did not go to the van every week, but sometimes we would meet the great, red-cheeked seamen of Gometra, returning home by way of a short-cut near our house, and they would set down their sacks and, delving into them, they would give us apples, as rosy as their faces, or biscuits or sweets. Cailleach Ruaraidh, too, passing our house on her way home from the van would hand me a bar of toffee. One of my most abiding memories of the people of Mull is of their kindness to children.

Whether we went to the van or not, each Saturday Allan Dally brought us four quartern loaves, baked by Yules of Tobermory, and we would go on foot or by boat to the ferry to collect them. The loaves were not wrapped as they are nowadays, and sometimes the temptation to nibble the delicious newly baked bread, with its 'black' and 'white' (well-baked and lightly-baked) ends, proved irresistible, so that, by the time we reached home, one of the loaves would bear the marks of our depredations. The loaves kept well for the whole week and none was wasted.

In addition to the baker's bread, my mother baked on a griddle oatcakes and a variety of scones – soda scones, potato scones, treacle scones, little round scones with currants, and scones made with a sprinkling of Indian meal mixed in the flour. She also made pancakes on the griddle.

The main supply of groceries was bought in bulk from MacFarlane Shearer, Greenock, and conveyed direct from there to Ulva pier by a smart little steam coaster with a cream-coloured smokestack, the Brenda, which plied from the Clyde to the Islands once a month. A typical half-yearly order would include bolls of flour, oatmeal, Indian corn (for the hens); boxes of tea, bags of sugar and salt, tins of biscuits; tinned foods, to be kept in reserve for visitors who might arrive unexpectedly – Fray Bentos Corned Beef, Libby's Ox-tongue, John West Salmon, Bartlett's Pears; packets of cereals for milk puddings – sago, semolina, rice, Brown and Polson's Cornflour. From time to time the order would include 'luxuries' such as Lyle's Golden Syrup, treacle, Nestlés Condensed Milk, Coleman's Mustard and H.P. Sauce. The large bottle of boiling sweets, sometimes included in the order, was kept, locked up, in my father's press and the sweets rationed out, two or three a day, until the bottle was empty.

MacCullochs, the butchers in Oban, sent us by post fresh butcher meat – mince, stewing steak and, for the Sunday dinner, beef which was boiled and from which my mother would make broth. On a cold winter's Sunday, the prospect of returning from church (there was no form of heating in it) to this comforting meal was very pleasing, and with a small boy's literal interpretation of metaphysical language I concluded that this was what the fourth beatitude was all about: 'Blessed are they which do hunger and thirst after righteousness; for they shall be filled.'

Hugh MacInnes, Kilbrennan, was the only farmer in the district that I remember keeping pigs. When he killed a pig he would bring us a joint of pork – chops or a ham, uncured, which when fried, provided us with a gourmet meal, the gastronomic highlight of the year. When my father attended meetings of the presbytery of Mull in Salen he sometimes bought in D.P. Ferguson's shop Palethorpe's pork sausages, and these fried, sizzling, golden brown and delicious, challenged the Kilbrennan pork for top place in our culinary order of merit. Apart from the butcher meat from Oban and the pork from Kilbrennan, the only other fresh meat we had during winter was rabbit which we had for dinner, stewed with vegetables, once a week. A pair of rabbits cost eight old pence and by saving the skins till the end of the season, we could get a few pennies for them from Barney Long, who made a living by collecting rabbit and other skins in the islands and mainland of Argyll.

A large part of our winter diet consisted of salt fish and meat. At the back-end we got a firkin of salt herring and a large, split, dried and salted ling. These salted fish provided our dinners for two days each week. The ling was suspended from a nail in the kitchen wall. When required it was taken down, dusted and fillets were cut off by the household handsaw – it was as hard as board – and soaked in cold water overnight to remove excess salt. They were boiled and serve with boiled potatoes and a white parsley sauce.

Also at the beginning of winter we bought a sheep from Hugh MacInnes, Kilbrennan, who came with it personally and slaughtered it in our byre. The blood and innards were prepared by my mother for making the black and white puddings (marag dhubh, marag gheal) which we regarded as delicacies. Apart from one or two cuts which were cooked fresh, the rest of the carcase was cut into pieces and packed in a wooden tub with coarse salt and left there until it was thoroughly cured and pickled. The boiled salt mutton and boiled potatoes were on the menu one day in the week throughout the winter.

It was not only our provisions that had to be imported from outside the island. The peatbanks had become depleted long before we arrived in Ulva and fuel for lighting and heating had to be brought from the south. Coal was delivered by puffers. I remember the *Starlight* which, being flat-bottomed, was able to discharge its cargo when beached at low tide. The coal was delivered from the puffer to the house by carts – a cart-load was reckoned to be a ton of coal. Roderick MacNeill with his mare Irene was the carter who delivered our coal. In Coille a' Mhinisteir, at the back of our house, we collected dried twigs for kindling and fallen branches which we cut into logs with a two-handed saw, but the black iron range on which the cooking was done required to be fuelled by coal in order to operate effectively. For lighting we had paraffin oil lamps, single-wicked, double-wicked and, for outdoor use at night, a storm lantern, and these were filled with paraffin from a barrel mounted on a stand outside which was imported from the mainland.

15

What We Ate – Home-grown Products

THE SHOP-BOUGHT PROVISIONS were supplemented by home-grown products. The walled garden, well manured, produced our year's supply of potatoes and other vegetables. We grew Golden Wonder potatoes, one or other of the varieties introduced by MacKelvie of Arran, such as Arran chief, Arran banner, Arran pilot, and potatoes with bright blue skins called Kerry blues. Potatoes were boiled in their skins and eaten sometimes with a pat of butter, or peeled and boiled and mashed and eaten with milk. Left-over boiled potatoes were sliced and crisply fried – the nearest we got to the ubiquitous chips and crisps of later years. One Christmas, we got a parcel from a friend containing gifts for the family. The gifts were packed in a tin box on which was written 'Golden Wonder Potato Crisps'. Since the tin looked to me like a container for biscuits or sweets, I wondered what toffees or biscuits made out of potatoes tasted like.

In the garden we grew cabbages, turnips, carrots, leeks, parsley, beetroot and rhubarb. To combat the depredations made on the cabbages by the caterpillars of the cabbage white butterfly, we used a solution of soot and water. The old crab apple tree produced good crops of apples every year without any attention whatsoever and my mother used any apples that survived our raids to make apple or apple and bramble jelly. She was also responsible for the cultivation of flowers – daffodils, narcissi, old-fashioned roses, montbretia and fuchsia – which flourished in the wet mild climate.

One half of the garden was made into a hen-run where our poultry had free range. When eggs were plentiful some were placed in an earthenware jar and preserved in water-glass, a kind of gelatine originally obtained from sturgeons' bladders from which its other name, isinglass, is derived. Eggs were eaten boiled, scrambled, fried or poached. They were used in baking and for pancakes. Switched egg and cream was considered very nutritious and easily digested. There was, however a saying that I heard in Mull and nowhere else, 'There is nothing as dangerous as an egg'. Whether this was a pre-Edwina Currie salmonella scare or some superstitious taboo, I do not know. When eating boiled eggs, the horn spoon should be dipped in ash or salt. One family I knew dispensed with either, and used sugar instead. The person who told me about the saying quoted above, the late Seonaidh Russell, Salen, also quoted a Gaelic proverb which I have not seen or heard elsewhere:

Ubh gun ìm, gun luath, gun salann,
'n ceann seachd bliadhna gun tig galar.

An egg without butter, without ash, without salt,
at the end of seven years, disease will come.

The white of an egg is the ingredient of many traditional folk cures.

The first poultry we kept were white and black leghorns, smallish birds with glossy feathers, the cockerels very handsome with colourful plumage. Later, they were replaced by a heavier breed, Rhode Island reds. Once, one of these hens had her leg broken in a trap set for a rat, and was the subject of an amateur veterinary experiment. My father splinted and plastered the limb, using a bandage steeped in a paste of flour and water. We kept her in the house and fed her by hand for a week or two, hoping the fracture would heal. It did, but left her with a stiff leg that caused her to limp which earned for her the name 'Steppy'. Thereafter, she forsook her own kind and followed us about, like our dogs and cats, wherever we went, keeping up a continuous, companionable conversation of clucking noises.

Another of the Rhode Island reds was the subject of a kind of genetic experiment. A clutch of ducks' eggs was put under the broody hen which was quite happy to sit on them. When, however, the eggs did not hatch at the time hens' eggs normally would, she began to show some signs of anxiety. She continued sitting for a further week and her perseverance was rewarded when, one by one, the little ducklings emerged from the shells. She led them out with pride, seemingly unaware that her offspring had decidedly un-hen-like bills and feet. But one day, after heavy rain, when she led them out, her little charges spied the puddles of water left by the rains and made for them as fast as their little webbed feet could carry them and plunged in, leaving their hapless mother clucking distractedly on the shore of their little loch. We have a Gaelic proverb which explains why the little ducklings behaved as they did: 'Theid dualchas an aghaidh nan creag' or, as they say in English, 'Heredity will out'.

We had a pair of white doves which roosted in a

plywood tea chest that hung from the wall outside the kitchen window. They contributed nothing to the larder but, rather, were consumers of large quantities of the grain given to the hens. All day they kept up a continuous throaty cooing. 'What are they saying?' we would ask, and my father would explain that they were speaking to one another in Gaelic and saying, 'Cha b'ann de mo chuideachd thu!' 'You do not belong to my people!') If you are not a Gaelic speaker, ask one who is to repeat the phrase rapidly three times, and you will, indeed, hear that this is what the doves were saying!

We had a small rowing boat called *The Duchess of Rothesay*, after one of the Clyde paddlesteamers. On summer and autumn evenings we fished in Loch-a-Tuath with homemade fishing tackle – a rod made from a trimmed larch branch or sapling with a line, gut and hook attached. We fastened lures, made from sea-gull feathers, to the hooks with cotton thread, and trolled for the surface-feeding varieties of fish such as cuddies (cudaig), saith (saoidhean) and, hopefully, lythe (liùthag), a golden brown fish with a sweet flavour. Returning home as the evening grew dusky and colder, we cleaned our catch and cast the offal overboard for another mouth that was waiting its share – a seal, too old or lazy to catch fish for himself, that followed a few feet behind us. By the time we arrived home, my mother would have the big iron pot, with milk, water and butter on the fire ready to cook our freshly caught supper – a meal fit for a king, I thought, the sweeter on account of having personally caught it.

More exotic dishes appeared on the menu from time to time: pheasant (easag), on one occasion, a curlew (guilb-neach), inadvertantly caught in a trap, razor-fish muirsgian), scallops (slige chreachain) and lobster (giomach).

At different seasons of the year, as we rambled along the roads, through the woods and by the shores, we would emulate our hunter/gatherer ancestors, picking and eating as we walked, bramble berries, black, sweet and juicy, wild raspberries and sometimes the tiny sweet wild strawberries that grew in the ditches by the road-side. In autumn we gathered hazelnuts from the copses and stored them till they were ripe and brown. We gathered whelks from the shores and boiled them in empty tin cans on fires made of dry bracken and twigs, eating the molluscs with the aid of my mother's hatpins.

The most exotic and unexpected addition to our fare came to us via our private letter box. In order to save the postman a detour when delivering our mail at the manse on his way to Gometra, my father received permission to erect a letter box some distance from our house at a point that lay on his route. One summer, when we were away on holiday, a swarm of bees entered the box through the slit for letters, and soon the whole interior was filled with honey-combs and honey. There was no shortage of helpers in plundering the hive, and the treasure was shared. It was the first time I tasted honey: the phrase, 'a land flowing with milk and honey' took on a new significance for me. The letter box had attached to it an enamelled metal plaque, with the government insignia, declaring that it was the property of the post-master general. He was not informed of the unusual use to which his property had been put.

16

The Minister's Cow

IN THE ORIGINAL PLAN of the H-shaped, single-storeyed manse of Ulva, designed by Thomas Telford, one wing was designated as a byre. This concept was an ingenious adaptation of the long, low black houses in which the crofter and his cattle lived under the same roof, to the mutual benefit of both. In the case of the Ulva manse this arrangement was not implemented; a byre was built separate from the house, and the apartment originally intended to house the minister's cow was used by us as a storeroom-cum-playroom where we, the children, kept our toys and books and bric-à-brac.

The minister's cow and a glebe to provide her winter fodder were essential elements in sustaining the economy of a country minister and his family. The Commissioners for Building Churches in the Highlands recognised this fact and ensured that the ministers of the parliamentary churches were provided with a manse and a glebe as well as with a guaranteed stipend. When the first minister of Ulva, the Rev. Neil Maclean, spent £17 of his own money

1. Sheila MacFadyen and her son Sandy: a studio portrait probably taken by Fred Scriven, Oban c. 1926. Sheila was the Laird's dairymaid, and she lived with her son in the last thatched house in Ulva. Sandy died of peritonitis in Oban, aged about nineteen, shortly after this picture was taken. Reproduced with permission from Mairi and Dianne Campbell, Craignure.

2. and 3. Sheila's cottage and old smiddy. Above, c. 1930 from Ulva Heritage centre brochure; below, restored and re-thatched. Reproduced with permission from C. Ann MacKenzie.

4. Manse, garden, church and glebe from the shore. Reproduced with permission from C. Ann MacKenzie.

5. Pulpit with sounding box. Reproduced with permission from C. Ann MacKenzie.

6. Old farm buildings incorporating part of the last chief of MacQuarries'
house where Dr Johnson and Boswell stayed in 1773. Reproduced with
permission from C. Ann MacKenzie.

7. Gometra school pupils. The two young men in the back row were probably students who taught during the summer months when there was no resident teacher, c. 1917. Reproduced with permission from The Isle of Mull Museum.

8. Gometra school. Madge MacLeod, teacher, Mrs MacDonald, Baile cloich, School cleaner and Lachie MacNeill, postman, c. 1926.

9. The pier at Ulva. Angus MacGillivray, ferryman, is on the pier. In the boat are church dignitaries with my father, second from the left, and MacInnes, Corkamull, seated third left, 1928. Taken from the family album.

10. The author and a friend, Perth, 1997.
Reproduced with permission from C. Ann MacKenzie.

to blast the rocky outcrops on the glebe, he was protecting his own interests and, indeed, those of the ministers, including my father, who succeeded him.

The important role of the minister's cow for us in Ulva was played by Lena, a cross Shorthorn-Ayrshire, a docile, intelligent creature, chosen for us by Colin Fletcher, the estate manager, who was renowned throughout the district for his knowledge of cattle and their cures. Although Lena was denied a place under our roof, as Telford intended, she was regarded by us as one of the family, and we spent a good deal of our time each day tending her – leading her to and from pasture on the Ardellum lands, mucking the byre and spreading hay for her bed, milking her morning and evening, and, during the summer, making hay in the glebe for her winter's keep.

These chores were not grudgingly performed; we enjoyed being involved in the daily round of country life and Lena amply repaid our attention to her by providing the milk and cream that we took with our morning porridge and milk puddings, that we made into butter and crowdie (gruth) that we spread on our pieces, that we mixed with oatmeal to make stapag and that provided us with curds and whey and buttermilk.

The only flaw in this bovine paragon was an addiction that she indulged once a year. Among the hazel copses in Coille a' Mhinisteir behind the manse, wild garlic (creamh) grew in profusion in early summer. Although these copses were not on the way we drove her to pasture, she would catch at a distance the alluring (to her) aroma, and nothing her small herds could do would restrain her from heading straight for the object of her desire nor drive her away from it until she had gorged herself on the tender pungent plants. For days afterwards her milk and its products were as garlic-flavoured as any Italian or Frenchman would have desired. For me, it was utterly off-putting and to this day, I have never been able to stomach any dish flavoured with garlic.

Every year Lena produced a calf to which we gave romantic names – Dealbhach (Picturesque), Bruce, Wallace, Fionn. My task, as a small boy, at calving was to induce the newly-born calf to suck his mother's milk from a pail. I held the pail between my knees, and when I got his head into the milk, I put my fingers into his mouth. After much bucking, head-butting and sneezing on the calf's part, I could feel my hand being sucked so strongly that I began to fear that my whole arm would be sucked down his hungry gullet. By the end of the operation, one third of the milk had found its way inside him, one third had spilled onto the floor and one third had spattered on to my clothes and person.

It was a tearful fay for the family when the calf left to be sold at the sale in Salen, but the five or seven pounds which Lena's calves fetched was a useful addition to the family finances.

I remember, one summer, Lena became ill and, as there was no vet in Mull at that time, we relied on those, like Colin Fletcher, who were knowledgeable about cattle, for advice. While the case was being considered, a suggested cure came from an unexpected source. Anna Dhubh, who was a frequent visitor at the manse, and who had probably the best store of traditional Gaelic lore and songs in all the parish, advised my mother what she should do: take the church key, go round Lena three times in a sunwise direction (deiseil), invoking the name of the Trinity. Millennia of religious beliefs and superstitions were encapsulated in this formula: the magical powers of iron, sun worship, the mystical power of some numbers and the comparatively recent Christian faith were all invoked to cure the minister's cow. I do not know for certain whether my mother followed Anna Dhubh's advice or if Colin had hit upon a cure, but I do know that Lena fully recovered.

Lena and her calves, the hens, ducklings and doves were all part of the household, members of the family, you might say. So, too, were the dogs, all called Dileas (Faithful), that succeeded one another as pets – a Yorkshire terrier that features in a studio photograph of Mairi and Angus as children in Rothesay; a black Labrador cross and a Cairn terrier. Of the two cats carried by them in cardboard boxes on our arrival at Ulva, Manxy, the black Manx cat, disappeared early on. We suspected that it was mistaken for a black rabbit and met the fate reserved for what Sir Donald Monro, Dean of the Isles, called 'cunings' at the hands of rabbit trappers. But Percy survived for many years and, despite its masculine name, became the matriarch of a long line of cats – Kitty, Nancy, Tommy and Grizzel. I have a vivid memory of the scene in the byre at milking time on a cold, dark winter evening, lit by the storm lantern, Lena in her stall contentedly chewing the cud and, in a row at the very verge of the sheuch, a line of cats, each with its little enamel dish, queueing up in order of seniority under the matriarchal eye of Percy, for their share of the milk.

17

'The People of the Ulva Parish are Very Healthy.'

THE CHAPTER HEADING IS taken from the *New Statistical Account of 1843*, prepared by F.W. Clark. The same could be said of the people of Ulva during the 1920s. We and our fellow islanders enjoyed a high standard of health, despite the high levels of salt in our diet. Colds, mild stomach upsets, earache, chilblains, just about made up the catalogue of childhood ailments; measles, whooping cough, chicken-pox we contracted long after leaving Ulva. Grown-ups had rarely any more serious complaints than toothache and rheumatism. I was myself an adult before I heard the word cancer or àillse, the Gaelic for it, for the first time.

Our doctor, Dr Reginald MacDonald, lived in Salen and his visits to 'this outpost of his wide district' were more social calls than professional attendances. I do not recall seeing a district nurse, but I assume that there was one in Salen. A news item in the *Oban Times*, dated 19/1/24, reports that Mrs Melles of Gruline organised a bargain sale of work at Ulva school for the nursing fund.

Nursing associations were set up in districts to support the district nurses and raise money to improve their living conditions and to provide means of transport.

Another item of news from the same report gives a pleasing account of an old woman that I remember. She was the mother of Sandy Black, the mail contractor and car hirer who to me seemed an old man:

> One of the oldest inhabitants in Mull is Mrs Black, Oskamull, who is now in her ninety-sixth year. She is still in possession of all her faculties and takes a keen interest in everything connected with the welfare of the people of the parish. Daily she may be seen out of doors attending to the needs of her poultry or seated on a stool in front of her cottage enjoying the fresh breeze from Ben More across Loch-nan-keal.

With longevity the norm, the death of a young person was profoundly shocking to children under the delusion that only the very aged died. In Mull Gaelic usage, the word bàs (death) or bàsaich (die) applied to animals. Sheep and cows 'died'; people 'departed' (dh'fhalbh e) or 'travelled' (shiubhail e) or 'changed' (chaochail e). The death of a young man as a result of disease or an accident was regarded as 'untimely'.

Calum Ruaraidh, the eldest son of the family who lived in Ardellum Lodge, had served in the Royal Navy during the Great War and returned home having contracted tuberculosis. There was no cure for TB at that time and it was highly contagious. Sufferers were more or less isolated from the community and sometimes lived in outdoor cabins with their own dishes and utensils. In Lewis, where most of my relatives lived, TB was rife. If we received a letter from a relative in whose household there was a patient the letter was opened and read in the open air and burnt immediately after perusal. We called the disease by its Gaelic name 'a'chaitheamh' ('the wasting') and when we did we spoke it in a whisper. I believe that Calum was a victim of the First World War although his name does not appear on the Ulva War Memorial.

Some years after Calum's death, another young man from Ulva, Sandy Sheila, whom we knew well, took ill with appendicitis. He was taken to the Oban hospital for an operation but he died of peritonitis. He would have been about nineteen or twenty. Another young lad we used to see in Salen where his father was the piermaster, MacRae, died in tragic circumstances long remembered in the island. On the night of the Oban Games, the *Grenadier* went on fire alongside the pier at Oban. Young MacRae was trapped below decks and perished. He was a cabin boy on the ill-fated vessel. Her skipper, Captain Cameron, an Iona man, also lost his life in the disaster.

Funeral services were conducted by the minister at the door of the house of the deceased, the coffin resting on two wooden chairs placed outside the door, with the neighbours gathered round in the open air. The cortège was borne on a cart and accompanied to the graveside by men only. The grave was dug on arrival and filled in and returned after the interment. Afterwards, the mourners, sheltering in the lea of the graveyard wall were served by members of the bereaved family with a glass of whisky (all were served from the same glass) and biscuits and cheese. Never having been personally present at a funeral in Ulva, I rely on what I was told to describe the proceedings, but I remember going to meet my father on his way home from a funeral and getting from him his share of the biscuits and cheese which he took home for us in his coat pocket – water biscuits and red cheddar cheese which we called, macabresquely, 'the remains of the funeral'.

There was no resident dentist in Mull at that time. I was twenty-one when I first sat in a dentist's chair. We cleaned our teeth with a rag dipped in salt or soot from the back of the grate. When I was about eight or nine I got my first toothbrush and a round aluminium tin containing a pink, freshly-flavoured block of Gibb's Dentifrice accompanied by a little illustrated booklet that told the story of how the 'Ivory Castles' were defended against the villain 'Giant Decay'.

We had our own home cures for minor ailments and afflictions; cuts and scratches were cleaned with methylated spirit before iodine was introduced to the medical chest. Later, iodine was replaced by a pleasant-smelling ointment called Germoline. Whisky was used externally and internally for earache and 'gumboils' and, mixed with sugar and water, for colds and stomach upsets. Docken leaves gave fast relief from nettle stings; chilblains were soothed by dipping affected fingers and toes in the water in which potatoes were boiled, or by plunging them into snow when available. The chafing of boys' thighs caused by short trousers was eased by blonaig – chicken fat melted down. This chafing was most prevalent during the dry, cold, windy March weather, hence our name for it, màrtanaich. Bread poultices were applied to bealing sores on the feet, a common occurrence in summertime when we went about bare-footed treading on thorns and jagged rocks.

18

The Clothes We Wore

AMONG THE 604 PEOPLE living in Ulva in 1837 there were weavers, shoemakers and tailors so that they could all be clad and shod respectably without leaving their own homes. There were no such amenities in the parish when I remember it. The women, however, still knitted the socks, stockings, jerseys, scarves, mittens and even woollen moccasins for indoor wear for the whole household. During her leisure hours, my mother was never without her knitting needles, and I remember her saying that Sunday always felt longer than other days because she had 'nothing to do with her hands'. Although the strict Sabbatarianism enjoined in the Outer Isles was not imposed on our family, or, indeed, in Mull generally, knitting was one activity that did not fall within the category of 'acts of necessity and mercy' which could legitimately be performed on the Sabbath. Incidentally, whistling on the Sabbath (feadaireachd air là na Sàbaid) was also proscribed, and it took a complicated feat of modulation for a small boy to convert the lively strathspey, 'The Devil's in the Kitchen' into the plaintive, minor key of 'Coleshill' halfway through the rendering. Whistling psalm tunes was permissible: whistling pipe tunes was not. I have read that in the north-east of Scotland, the fast day before Communion Sunday was called 'Whistlin' or 'Fusslin' Sunday' because the fast day was kept like a Sunday except that whistling secular tunes was permitted.

When Angus was born the family was given a Singer sewing machine by a friend. It was my father, not my mother, who learned how to work 'Angus' sewing machine', as we called it. He made trousers for us boys with it, using cloth from his discarded suits, and, in the few family photographs that survive from our Ulva years, his tailoring skills are recorded. Another photograph, taken in 1926, shows Angus, Stewart and myself dressed in full Highland dress, bought for us by another Rothesay friend.

Like all other boys and girls we went barefoot from the beginning of June till the beginning of September. It was a ritual of childhood: the cult of bare-footedness which, bealing sores notwithstanding, we observed and practised.

On Sundays and special occasions all, young and old, were smartly turned out; the men in navy-blue serge suits and wearing collars and ties, farmers and lairds usually wearing tweed plus-four suits and very occasionally kilts and jackets.

The older women wore costumes with ankle-length skirts and long, waisted jackets, blouses fastened to the neck, their hair combed severely back and gathered into a bun behind their heads. They wore velour or straw hats decorated with brightly coloured wax flowers and berries, even birds, jauntily perched atop their heads and secured by long hatpins with ornamental heads thrust through their buns. They did not alter their wardrobes with the vagaries of fashion, and in the late twenties some of them wore the same fashions, indeed, the same costumes that they wore prewar.

With girls and young women it was quite different. The English mail order firms, such as Oxendale's and J.D. Williams, brought about a revolution in women's fashions. Two or three times a year a glossy catalogue from Oxendale would arrive by post. The garments were illustrated with pen and ink sketches with descriptions and prices under them. To me this made most boring reading, page after page of dresses that to me looked identical, the only feature of interest being a replica of a postal order with detailed instructions as to how it and its counterfoil should be filled in.

To the younger women and girls, however, Oxendale's catalogue afforded hours of entertainment and discussion. Having agonised over the goods on offer and having finally sent in their order with the postal order, obtained through the postman, they waited with keen anticipation for the arrival of the dress or costume or coat that was to be their Sunday best for the ensuing year. By this means, the Jessies and Maggies of Ulva were as modishly dressed as the Sallies and Pollies of London or Manchester.

Ulva, in 'the roaring twenties' had its 'flappers'; young women in knee-length skirts with flounced hems, silk stockings, strapped shoes, with bobbed or shingled hair, wearing cloche hats or bandeaux. In the old family album there are wedding photographs of young cousins from Scalpay, Harris, wearing wedding dresses in this style.

The new fashions, needless to say, were frowned on by the older generation of women and, from the pulpits of the more traditional churches, ministers fulminated against the new look and the mail order firms that purveyed it. One Free Presbyterian minister in Skye, well known for his *obiter dicta* on the subject, one Sunday gave out his text from the book of the minor prophet Habakkuk, and waited with ill-concealed impatience while the members of his congregation thumbed through their Bibles in an effort to locate the obscure prophet. 'Ah!' he said at last, 'If it had been J.D. Williams' catalogue you would have found the place before now!' ('A, nam b'e leabhar J.D. Williams a bh'ann 's fhada bho'n a bha e air a bhi agaibh!')

My father had his suits made by tailors who specialised in clerical attire but he had his boots made by the bootmaker in Salen, Charles Maclean, an Greusaiche. I remember him coming to deliver the boots personally and Angus and I going to the ferry to convoy him to the manse. He had a white beard, twinkling blue eyes and a good way with children. On the road home we took him aside to show him a gooseberry bush, doubtless a seedling from the laird's garden, which we had discovered. He was impressed by our find and he told us that they had gooseberries in Salen too; would we like to try the Salen gooseberries? he asked. Surprised, we said we would. His eyes twinkling, he delved into his coat pocket and produced a poke of sugared almonds, pink, mauve, blue. To this day, when I see sugared almonds in a shop, I think of them as Salen gooseberries.

Teàrrlach an Greusaiche was not only paid for his excellent craftsmanship, my father also composed a song extolling the bootmaker and his products – a sort of forerunner of the jingles you hear nowadays on TV commercials. I can remember one verse of it:

Nam biodh paidhear aig MacLeòid dhiubh,
Chuireadhdh iad òirleach air 's a' chrannaig.

If MacLeod had a pair of them,
They would add an inch to his stature in the pulpit.

MacLeod was the minister of Salen at the time and he was a small man.

19

The Process of Learning

WHEN THE CHURCH WAS built in 1827 there were two schools in Ulva – a parochial school and a school supported by the Scottish Society for the Propagation of Christian Knowledge, one of the so-called Charity Schools, and there was a school in Gometra. By 1918, the parish school was on the Mull side of the ferry – Ulvaferry school, with a side school in Gometra and one at Fanmore.

The schoolmaster at Ulvaferry when we arrived in Ulva was Alexander Shanks whom I do not remember but I remember Dan Neil MacColl, Torloisg, who succeeded him. A cutting from the *Oban Times* reports a treat organised by him at which:

a Christmas tree, gifted by Mr and Mrs Keele of Killiechronain who motored specially to the school with it was a welcome innovation. The children and their parents packed the school to the utmost capacity. The school was decorated and the tree, loaded with innumerable toys, presented a magnificent sight. Mr Lachlan MacNeill, Oskamull, impersonated Santa Claus and presented each child with presents from the tree. Tea was served by Miss MacColl, the Schoolhouse, Miss MacColl, Fanmore, Miss Mary J. MacNeill and Miss MacFadyen, Oskamull Farm. Cake and fruit were also served to the company, and ample justice was done by the children to the good things provided for them. Present among the guests were, Mr Donald MacColl, the veteran keeper to Captain Compton, Master Francis Clark of Ulva, Mrs MacKenzie and Miss Mairi MacKenzie, the Manse. Mr Malcolm MacPhail proposed a vote of thanks to the teacher and committee who organised the treat and expressed the hope that it would become an annual institution at Ulvaferry.

Dan Neil MacColl was succeeded by Mrs Naomi Campbell, a widow with four of a family, a native of Barvas, Lewis. Her niece, Miss Madge MacLeod, was the teacher at Gometra, and she often called at the manse on her way by bicycle to and from Gometra at weekends when she stayed with her aunt. Madge later succeeded her aunt as teacher at Ulvaferry school.

The people of the parish were well served by the successive teachers, not only for their professional skills but also for their contributions to the social and cultural interests of the community. Of the children in the parish during those years, five or six became teachers, one a doctor, one a minister, beside others who pursued successful careers in agriculture, at sea and in various trades.

None of the manse children attended Ulvaferry school

because that would involve crossing the ferry which, although short, could be hazardous for small children in stormy wintry weather and would also involve them in a fairly long walk to and from school each day. My father received official permission to educate us at home. He had, in the course of his training for the ministry, considerable experience of teaching in 'the ladies' schools' in many of the islands – his first teaching assignment was at Tor-an-eas, Mull. My first classroom was the parlour (the study) of Ulva manse, and I did not sit, as a pupil, at a school desk until I sat the qualifying examination at the age of about twelve at Ulvaferry school, under the watchful eye of Mrs Campbell and of Alasdair MacDonald, Laggan, who was the invigilator. I was the only candidate that year. I received all my primary education at home.

We sat on chairs round the big table, covered with a chenille drape that fell over the edges almost to the floor, doing our sums and practising our writing on slates. We also practised writing with pen and ink in our copy books. These books had proverbs printed in beautiful copper-plate lettering and, below each proverb, there were six blank lines on which we attempted to copy the original specimen, avoiding 'pothooks', crooked down strokes beneath the line in letters f, g, p, q, y and z.

The rules of English grammar, syntax, spelling and punctuation were drilled into us; sentences were analysed – subject, predicate and object, words were parsed. We learned by rote multiplication tables, poetry and prose passages, psalms and the shorter catechism. We wrote essays on outings, events, places and people. A favourite opening to an essay could be 'The day being fine, we went for a picnic.' The words 'got' and 'nice' were discouraged: 'I got your letter' – No – 'I received your letter' – Yes. 'It was a nice day' – Wrong; 'It was a fine day' – Right. A split infinitive was forbidden and you must never end a sentence with a preposition. We had readers – *The Royal Crown Readers* that had selections of poems and prose passages to provide us with models of correct English usage.

My father taught us arithmetic as he, himself, had been taught it as a boy, by the method known as Gray's arithmetic. In the David Livingstone museum at Blantyre there is a copy of David's arithmetic book with his name and addition sums in his own handwriting on the inside cover. The book is *An Introduction to Arithmetic* by James Gray, the twenty-second edition, 1825. Teaching methods change from generation to generation and none, perhaps, more radically than those used in teaching mathematics; so that when I attempted the first term arithmetic examination in the first year secondary at Oban High School my outdated workings were not acceptable to 'Scrim', our maths teacher, and I was given the belt for my pains.

But at home we were introduced to two other branches of mathematics: algebra and Euclid, the latter was known as geometry in the school curriculum. Fortunately the way I was taught algebra and Euclid was not fundamentally different, apart from the latter's name, to Scrim's way and so I avoided further acquaintance with his favourite teaching aid.

My father thought it fit and proper that Latin should be taught at primary level and the quiet afternoons in Ulva manse resounded with new mantras. Instead of 'manschiefend' and 'two-times-two-is-four' there was '*amo, amavi, amatum amare*' and '*dominus, domine, domini, dominum, domino, domino*'. We practised our new-found linguistic skills at mealtimes: '*Ubi est puella?*'

'*Hic est puella.*' By the time I was about ten or eleven, I had read a simplified version of Caesar's *Gallic War*.

Many years afterwards, Donald Morrison, the great seanchaidh of the Ross of Mull, told me that, as a boy, he knew an old man who could read Latin as 'well as a minister' because he had attended in his youth a Latin school in Mull. It was the first time I heard about such a school and I later found out that at Aros in the late eighteenth century there was one of the four Latin schools which were supported upon the Royal Bounty. The schoolmaster there had a salary of £25 a year and about thirty scholars attended. He taught English and writing, Latin and Greek and the elements of mathematics and bookkeeping.

History and geography were subjects in our curriculum, but art and science were not. Angus and I, however, enjoyed drawing and painting, using any available scrap of paper and the pencils, crayons and paintboxes that we got as Christmas presents. Not surprisingly, we dropped science after the third year and opted for Higher art. After school Angus graduated from the Edinburgh College of Art and became an art teacher.

The omission of any science subject from the curriculum left a void that we sought to fill by observation, experiment and listening to folk tales. When the glebe was scythed, small creatures were uncovered – frogs of many colours and beautiful legless lizards. These lizards, grotesquely misnamed slow worms or blind worms, are not worms nor are they blind or slow and, because of their shape, we believed them to be snakes and as such were to be killed. There were adders in Ulva that were venomous and the harmless lizards suffered on account of their superficial likeness to them. We believed that the wild cat had a barb in its tail which could inflict a serious wound on anyone rash enough to touch it.

I once decided to put another bizarre piece of country lore to the test. I was told that if you placed a hair from a horse's tail in a sluggish stream, with one end anchored in place with a stone, it would in time develop into a live eel. Not having access to a horse's tail, I tried out the experiment with a hair from Lena's tail and kept watch. After some time, as it became covered in slime and wriggled with the slow-running movement of the water, it did, indeed, give every appearance of being a live eel, but I was not convinced that it was the real thing. Perhaps our theory about eider ducks' nests was more scientifically sound. We observed that these ducks built their nests at the water's edge with the lowest part just above highwater mark but sufficiently near the sea's surface to ensure that the eggs were kept damp enough to ensure their hatching.

20

Entertainments and Pastimes

THE PROCESS OF LEARNING was not restricted to the hours spent at the chenille-covered table in the study, but continued during the long, dark evenings when the family gathered round the fire and passed the time in homemade entertainments.

We listened as our parents told us about their own childhood experiences, about their own parents and forebears in Lewis and Harris. We learned about the conditions that prevailed in the islands over a hundred years previously, of the struggles and hardships and of the fortitude and resourcefulness with which they were met. We heard of an ancestor who returned from the Napoleonic Wars with a soldier's knife (corc) and a pension of £5 a year and how, when taking a short-cut from the shore to his croft through the glebe, he was attacked by the minister's bull. It was a case of kill or be killed, and the old soldier stabbed the animal with his corc. The minister, enraged by the loss of his prized bull, took steps to deprive Angus of his pension. But the old veteran fought back: he took the packet to Ullapool and walked from there, every step of the way, to London where he appeared before the 'Green Table' ('am Bòrd Gorm') in Whitehall where he appealed successfully for the restoration of his pension.

We heard, too, of how my father's parents were evicted from the machair lands on the west of Harris where their forebears had lived for generations by the Earl of Dunmore, who owned South Harris at that time. We heard, not without some pride, that our grandfather was arrested for resisting the military – he flung a peat clod at one of the redcoats that were sent to enforce the evictions.

We listened to stories and legends about Mull's past – 'Eòghain a' chinn bhig' ('The Headless Rider') and 'Ailean nan Sop' ('Allan of the Straw'), the founder of the Macleans of Torloisg. We heard fairy stories and horror stories about the dreaded Eachuisge ('the Water-Horse') that could assume human and animal forms to lure unsuspecting maidens, usually at the shielings, to their doom.

Sometimes we were joined by visitors who contributed to the entertainment by singing, playing instruments and telling stories. As the hours sped by long past bedtime, I used to creep under the table, hidden by the overhanging table cover, to avoid being sent to bed and there I would listen, unnoticed and unseen, to the songs and music and the enthralling yarns, comic or blood-curdling, that were told.

At these evening entertainments my father would play Gaelic airs and pipe tunes on his fiddle and he would take *The Beauties of Gaelic Poetry* and sing the Gaelic songs of the great eighteenth century poets – Alasdair mac Mhaighstir Alasdair, Donnchadh Bàn and Uilleam Ros, or from Sinclair's Oranaiche and other collections the songs of the nineteenth century township bards and of his contemporaries – Neil MacLeod, Skye, Murdo MacLeod, Lewis, and the Mull bards – Dugald MacPhail, John MacFadyen and Livingstone of Crogan.

My mother had snatches of older traditional songs. The first song I remember hearing was the refrain from a sixteenth century song known as the Glenlyon Lament which she sang to me as an infant as a dandling song – 'Bà, bà mo leanabh' and later, the chorus of an eighteenth century Badenoch song, 'Bealach a' Ghàraidh'. But one of our favourite songs in her reportoire was a Lowland Scots ballad which she had picked up as a child in Lewis. In its transit across the Minch it had suffered a sea-change, as the following verse shows:

> A lady was in her garden walking,
> When a handsome sailor came passing by.
> He reviewed as he seized up to her
> And said, 'My dear, would you fancy I?'

I never did find out what the third line of the original was; perhaps it would be less intriguing than the Lewis version.

Gaelic conundrums, tongue-twisters and guessing games formed part of the fireside entertainments. One guessing game was accompanied by a Gaelic rhyme:

H-aon a mhicean, hàn a bhuicean
Maide-sùirn, cùl an dùirn
Seall romhad 's as do dhéidh
Cia meud adairc th'air a' bhoc?

Little son, little buck
Kiln-flue, back of fist
Look before you, look behind
How many horns has the buck?

This was recited as you submitted the top of your head to the knuckles of another player's fist. At the end of the last line the knuckle wielder would raise a number of fingers or none at all and you had to guess how many. If you guessed wrongly all the participants would join in the skull-knuckling.

I do not know when I became consciously aware that two distinct languages, Gaelic and English, were being spoken. I do not know whether I first heard, 'Dùin an dorus' or 'Shut the door'. People spoke or sang in Gaelic or English and I understood, as far as my limited powers of comprehension went, what the words meant without translating from one language to the other. My contemporaries in Ulva have told me that they had very little English until they went to school; Gaelic was their first language, their mother tongue, English was their second. In my case, the two languages developed simultaneously and seldom, if ever, did the two modes of speech get mixed up.

My father did not teach us Gaelic formally as he taught us English and Latin, although he was well qualified to do so. His father was unable to read or write Gaelic or English, but his mother had learned to read Gaelic, probably in one of the charity schools in Harris, and on Sunday afternoons she would take him ben the house, with her Gaelic Bible and a bag of tea fastened by a string round her waist. They took tea together and pored over the pages of the Bible, verse by verse and chapter by chapter, until, by the time that he was six years of age, he had read the Gaelic Bible from the first verse of Genesis to the last verse of Revelation. This was the foundation of his skill in writing the language which is evidenced in the many articles, short stories and poetry that were published in newspapers, magazines and books over the years.

102

Although he did not teach us Gaelic formally, he passed on to us the songs, rhymes and stories of our Gaelic heritage. He fulfilled his self-appointed task as educator by providing us with the fundamentals of an English education while passing on to us, in a less formal way, the rich cultural inheritance of our people. It had long been the view of legislators and educationalists that Gaelic should be 'abolished', 'removed', 'rooted out', extirpated' and replaced by English. My father evidently believed that it was not necessary to destroy the one in order to promote the other.

As part of our evening entertainment he would read aloud to us a chapter of one of Scott's Waverley novels and we enjoyed, and were encouraged, to read on our own such books as *Pilgrim's Progress*, *Uncle Tom's Cabin*, *David Copperfield*, *The Swiss Family Robinson*, *Little Women*, *Black Beauty*, *The Knights of the Round Table*, *A Basket of Flowers* (the first book I read from beginning to end), *The Boys' Own Paper*, Arthur Mee's *Children's Encyclopedia*.

We played ludo and draughts and card games. My favourite card game was 'catch the ten', a game played like whist except that the ten of the trump suit had a value of ten points. If you had the ten in your hand your main concern was to 'get it home' safely; if your opponent had it, you had 'to draw it' with a superior card.

One way or another, formally or informally, consciously or unconsciously, the process of learning was continuous.

21

Ceilidhs in the School at Ulvaferry

THE SCHOOL AT ULVAFERRY was the social centre for the community where we gathered for ceilidhs, informal concerts, presided over by Alasdair MacDonald, Laggan, Hugh MacInnes, Kilbrennan, or my father. Pipers, fiddlers and melodeon players provided the instrumental part of the entertainment and accompanied the dance which followed. Singers sang Gaelic and Scottish songs. One popular song I remember was in the form of macaronic verse with one half of a line in Gaelic, the other half in English –

Whiskers on a baby chan fhaca duine riamh!'

A popular performer of 'novelty acts' at the ceilidh was Màiri Phàraig, who played the trump (Jew's harp) and performed on paper and comb. She sang Gaelic songs of local provenance including a comic one about Bodach Chillbhrianain who had his beard cut off.

On one memorable occasion, a one-act play or sketch in English was performed, with Lachie, the post, playing the part of a minister, complete with clerical collar, stock and preaching bands borrowed from my father. It was a huge hit with the audience and, although I do not have the report of it which I am sure appeared in the *Oban Times*, I have no doubt it received high critical acclaim.

After the ceilidh, the schoolroom was cleared and the desks and other movable furnishings were carried out to the school playground. Before the advent of Slipperine, the rough floor boards were prepared for dancing by the application of soap flakes. Once, I was told, some mischievous spirit sprinkled cayenne pepper on the floor with dire results when the dancers engaged in the more robust steps of the *Schottische* or eightsome reel. The dust, laden with the pepper arose in clouds, the sound of sneezing all but drowning out the music. I was too young to stay for the dance but, Maggie of Cragaig, who often helped in the manse and who was not much older than Mairi, demonstrated with her the intricacies of the waltzes, two-steps and polkas that were then in vogue.

It could be said of the people of Mull, as it was said of the people of Islay, that they were fond of music and dancing – 'Bu toigh leo ceòl is dannsadh.' The dances held in the schoolhouse superseded the 'Dance of the Road' ('Dannsa an Rathaid') which my mother frequented as a young girl and which she described to me, and the schoolhouse ceilidh took the place of the gatherings around the fireside in the old black houses where tales were passed on from generation to generation and the old songs were sung in the old traditional manner. It was at the old black house ceilidh that Donald Morrison, as a boy, heard the marvellous tales which he was able to recite, word for word, when he was in his nineties, and I often heard him say, 'When the thatched houses went, the ceilidh went.' ('Nuair a dh'fholbh na taighean tughaidh, dh'fholbh an céilidh.')

It was not only in the choice of venues that Gaelic culture was changing. With the founding of An Comunn Gaidhealach in 1891 and the inauguration of the Mòd the following year, the style of Gaelic singing was being changed. There appeared a plethora of small songbooks with the tunes given in tonic sol-fa notation – An Smeòrach, An Uiseag, An Lòn-dubh. Choral arrangements in four-part harmony were published for the newly formed Gaelic choirs, and when Marjory Kennedy-Fraser (Marsalaidh nan Oran) published her *Songs of the Hebrides* in 1909, with elaborate piano accompaniment, they became immediately popular. The singing of Gaelic was being restyled and was being made more acceptable to the ears of the non-Gaelic audiences in the Lowlands. The early gold medalists at the Mòds, some of whom had trained in opera, produced records of their most popular numbers and these were eagerly bought.

An Comunn entered enthusiastically into the effort of bringing Gaelic singing into the mainstream musical norm, and, to this end, they sent out to the Gaelic heartlands singing teachers with a missionary zeal to teach us 'correct singing by the book'. One of those teachers was quickly dubbed 'Bodach an doh-ray'. Our teacher was Peggie MacDonald and we gathered in the Ulvaferry school, young and old, the adults squeezed into the children's desks, while she taught us the mysteries of the tonic sol-fa notation.

'Mi, doh, doh, soh, doh, doh', we would sing in strict time to her conducting, and when we had mastered the doh-ray-mis to her satisfaction, without scooping or individual ornamentation, we were permitted to sing the words:

Brochan lom, tana lom, brochan lom sùghain
Plain gruel, thin gruel, plain gruel of sowens

Puirt-a-beul, love-songs, laments were all taught with mathematical precision and and with serious earnestness by our dedicated mentor.

There were people attending the class, certainly in the parish, who knew the old Gaelic songs of Mull and could sing them in the traditional manner that had been handed down to them. Annie MacDonald (Anna Dhubh), Acharoinnich, was one of them. I used to listen to her as she sang them to my mother and I remember some of the verses she sang. Fortunately, there was living in Mull at that time an authority on Mull traditions, Counnduille Rankin Morrison who lived at Ceanngharair, near Dervaig. (I remember seeing him in church at Dervaig.) Anna Dhubh, once a year, walked from Acharoinnich to Ceanngharair to sing her songs to him. I have no doubt that her songs are preserved among those that appear in Counn's manuscript now deposited in the archives of the School of Scottish Studies, Edinburgh University.

I was learning that the process of learning sometimes involved the process of unlearning.

22

Piping and Pipers

THERE WERE SEVERAL PIPERS in the parish in our time and we heard about the famous pipers who lived there in the past. Counn Morrison, Ceanngharair, referred to earlier, was a descendant of the great dynasty of the Maclean pipers known as Clann Duiligh or Clann MhicRaing (Rankin), a family of Irish origin of the same stock as the Macleans of Mull. They settled in Kilbrennan and the first piper of the family was said to have received his art from the fairies at the Fairy Hill near Laggan Ulva. One of the family practised his art in secret in a cave hidden by the Easfors. The Rankins were on friendly terms with the MacCrimmons of Boreraig, and one of them, Duncan, married Seònaid, a daughter of one of the MacCrimmons who was, herself, a piper. When the Macleans of Duart lost possession of their lands in Mull to the Campbells of Argyll in 1692, the Clann Duiligh School of Piping continued without the support or patronage of the Campbell chiefs. Niall MacRaing, the last of the famous school, was piper to Maclean of Coll;

he played before Dr Johnson in Coll in 1773 and died there in 1819. His father, Eoghan, the last to teach at the Kilbrennan School of Piping, died at Kilbrennan in c.1783. When his other son, Hector, left Mull and went to live in Greenock in 1804, it was the first time in 500 years that Mull had no MacRaing piper playing there.

The history of Clann Duiligh and its famous pipers is well documented in contemporary Gaelic accounts and it is preserved, along with legendary elements, in the family traditions handed down through the generations. Neil Rankin Morrison, Kengharair, contributed a Gaelic paper to the Gaelic Society of Inverness, entitled, 'Clann Duiligh: Piobairean Chloinn-Ghill-Eathain' which is published in the transactions of the society, Vol. XXXVII, 1934. The brief summary given above is based on this paper.

The paper contains some interesting references to Archibald MacArthur and the MacArthur School of Piping in Ulva. Morrison acknowledges that Archibald was an excellent piper who won first prize for piping at the Highland Society Piping Competition in Edinburgh (elsewhere it is said he refused to accept the second prize at the competition of 1806, thinking he deserved first), but he had never heard of a school of piping in Ulva, until he read about it in a book about Mull written by John MacCormick. He refuted the suggestion, made by a John Johnston in Coll that the MacArthurs were pipers to the MacQuarries for several centuries. It was Ranald 'Staffa' MacDonald who sent MacArthur as a young lad to study piping under the MacCrimmons at Boreraig, and it was 'Staffa' MacDonald, too, who bought the Clann Duiligh two-droned bagpipes for the young piper. The pipes were restored to the family and were in the possession of the writer of the paper at the time of writing.

The John MacCormick (1870–1947) referred to in the paper, wrote Gaelic short stories and novels, and he compiled a series of sketches of Mull traditions under the title *The Island of Mull*. The following is an extract from it from which Morrison first heard of the MacArthur School of Piping in Ulva:

> At the tender age of nine or ten years, young MacArthur was placed, at the Marquis [sic] of Staffa's expense, in the MacCrimmon College at Dunvegan – the course lasted fourteen years . . . students came from various parts of Mull to attend his College at Ulva, and most of them were known to be players of high repute. The writer of these sketches, when a boy, remembers having seen an old piper who had received his tuition in the Pipers' College at Ulva. The race of pipers who for many years conducted the seminary long ago emigrated from their little island home; but memories of them are still green among the old natives of Mull.

Archibald MacArthur is mentioned by several visitors to Mull who recorded their impressions, and some of them are quoted by James McAnna in his pamphlet, 'The Ulva Families of Shotts'. Alexander Campbell, who toured the area in 1815 states that Archibald had been a pupil of Donald Ruadh MacCrimmon of Skye. (Donald Ruadh, the last of the MacCrimmons, died in 1825.) According to McAnna, Archibald MacArthur's Pipe College was located at Ormaig, Ulva. The croft was divided into four apartments: one for family use, one for receiving strangers, one for cattle and one for the use of students while practising.

Among the archives of the Isle of Mull Museum,

Tobermory, there is a hand-written letter, signed A.J. Macdonald, dated 26 April 1923, from Kilearnan Manse, Ross-shire, with some comments on the MacArthur pipers of Mull. The writer was the Rev. Dr Angus John Macdonald (1860–1932) who was minister of Kilearnan Parish Church. His manuscripts ('The Kilearnan Papers') are concerned with Gaelic lore and history, and he collaborated with the Rev. Dr Archibald Macdonald, Kiltarlity, in two important works on the MacDonalds, *The Clan Donald* and the *MacDonald Collection of Gaelic Poetry*. The letter was written in reply to a request from someone in Mull, unnamed, for information about the MacArthur pipers of Mull. In the letter Macdonald writes, 'I am more likely to receive from you more information than I can give you regarding the MacArthur pipers of Mull.' This suggests that the recipient of the letter must have been someone like Counn Morrison.

The letter continues: 'At the present moment I cannot remember anything about them except that one of them was piper to Ronald Macdonald of Staffa. I have a picture of him here in full Highland dress – a very great swell, and the date is 1810. I think I heard it said, or saw somewhere, that he had no connection with the Skye MacArthurs who were pipers to the Sleat family. Ronald of Boisdale no doubt found his piper in Mull. There were no MacArthur pipers in South Uist.' There follow notes about the Macintyre pipers to Clan Ranald. 'The Sleat family had a MacArthur piper in each parish of their estates.' (There was no Free Kirk in those days.) The letter goes on to give an account of the MacArthur pipers of the Sleat Macdonalds down the centuries.

In the concluding paragraph of this most interesting letter Macdonald writes: 'I am sorry not to be able to give you any light at all on the Mull MacArthurs. It was Colin Macdonald of Boisdale who in the second half of the eighteenth century bought the Mull lands, afterwards inherited by his son Ranald, by a third wife, who blossomed finally into Sir Reginald Seton Steuart of Allanton, Bt, dropping the Macdonald like a hot potato. Another son Col. Robert Macdonald lived on Inch Kenneth where he built a house.'

The 1810 picture of Archibald MacArthur in full Highland dress referred to in the letter in the National Library of Scotland in Edinburgh is reproduced on the back cover of McAnna's pamphlet.

One of the pipers I remember coming to our house to play for us was Duncan Campbell, the ploughman at Oskamull. He was nicknamed 'the Duke' for no better reason, as far as I knew, than that he was a Campbell. Like the great pipers of old he gave a name to his pipes – he called her Lucy. Lucy was a temperamental creature that demanded much attention before each performance. The hemp on the drone slides had to be dampened, the reeds and blowpipe valve had to be chewed, the bag had to be softened and made air-tight by the application of various concoctions ranging from sugar and water to white of egg and treacle. At length when Lucy's demands were satisfied the Duke would begin to play, marching up and down the cement kitchen floor, 'The Drunken Piper', 'Bonnie Ann', 'The Duke of Roxburgh's Farewell' to the 'Blackmount Forest'. I was enthralled. Not that he always succeeded in completing the tunes, Lucy's tantrums intervening. Then the Duke, modest, not to say self-deprecatory to a fault, would say, 'Chan eil agam ach criomagan.' ('I have only fragments.') He never blamed Lucy; he blamed his calling as a ploughman for any failure in execution. Grasping the iron plough handles tightly in cold weather stiffened the fingers and produced hacks (gàgan). Joiners and stone-masons who held their chisels and hammers firmly but with a more relaxed grip, he believed, made ideal pipers with their strong but supple fingers.

Unlike Lucy, the Duke's demands were very modest – frequent and copious cups of strong, sweet tea. From time to time throughout the course of an afternoon, he would indicate his need of refreshment with a set phrase – 'Tha pàthadh searbh orm.' (There is a bitter thirst on me). Tea, long stewed with milk and sugar was the essential accompaniment of all the social gatherings in the home where stories were told, songs sung and pipes and fiddles were played. To provide it was to pay a very modest price for the pleasure the performance gave us.

In dramatic contrast to the Duke and his beloved Lucy was another piper and his pipes who visited us in summer. This was Pipe Major William Gray of the City of Glasgow Police Band, one of the most distinguished pipers of the 1920s and '30s. He and Pipe Major William Ross, from Edinburgh, dominated the Piping Competitions at the major Highland gatherings. Both were inspirational teachers as well as performers and each of them compiled a tutor and collections of pipe tunes. William Gray used to spend his summer holiday at Oskamull farm with the MacFadyens – Mrs MacFadyen, Katie MacGregor before marriage, was, I believe, related to him. We could hear him play of an evening outside the farm, the music carrying clearly and sweetly across Loch-a-Tuath. He would spend an afternoon with us at the manse – a well set-up man, dressed in a tweed plus-four suit, with a genial affable manner, playing his magnificent, full silver-mounted bagpipes that, unlike Lucy, appeared to perform perfectly without the need of any cosseting.

113

At the end of one such visit he presented us with a practice chanter and a copy of his tutor which incorporated a drumming manual by Drum Major John Seton. I determined to master the mysteries of fingering so graphically illustrated in the book, and each evening one winter I sat beside the dying kitchen fire struggling on my own to translate the notation into the appropriate sounds on the chanter. I assumed that the first tune in the collection would be the easiest to learn. It was a tune I had never heard played, although now it must be about the best-known pipe tune there is – 'Scotland the Brave'. Laboriously and at length I was able to pick out the notes from the score.

Unfortunately, no-one was at hand to point out to me that the small notes were grace-notes and so I played them as full notes, thereby rendering the melody unrecognisable. The good pipe major, had he heard my rendering of 'Scotland the Brave', would, doubtless, applaud my diligence in perseverance, while his keen musical ear would have been offended by my dismal attempt.

23

The Telford Church at Ulva

THE ENCLOSED KIRKYARD IN which the church stood was not a burial ground and we, as children, used it as an extension of our playground. A row of trees at the south side included a mature monkey puzzle, the so-called Chile pine with its close-set clusters of prickly leaves. At the south-west corner there was a line of four or five trees, two of which were placed together at a distance just right to accommodate a swing. A cross post was secured to them from which the wooden seat of the swing was secured by ropes.

The church was of the T-shaped Telford design with no gallery. The layout of the interior was precisely adapted to the Presbyterian worship and practice in the West Highlands of the time. There was no baptismal font; baptisms were administered in the family home. There was no fixed altar or communion table; ministers, elders and communicants sat round a common table, boxed in from the rest of the pews, all on the same level. It was not designed to accommodate bridal parties; marriages were solemnised and celebrated in the family home of the bride. There was no space for the lying-in of the dead; funeral services were conducted at the family home and at the graveside. There was no organ or harmonium; the singing was led by a precentor standing in the precentor's box. At Gaelic services only metrical psalms were sung. The practice of 'giving out the line' solo by the precentor, still current in the outer Isles, was no longer used in Mull, if, indeed, it ever was. The function of the church bell was not to summon people from their homes, it was rung to intimate that the minister was approaching the church and to bid the members of the congregation waiting outside the building to extinguish their pipes and take their places inside. The tolling of the bell had the same function as an Introit or organ voluntary; it was a signal to prepare the people for public worship. The bell in Ulva's church was not housed in the belfry during our time but in one of the vestibules. When the church ceased to be used for regular worship the bell was gifted to the church extension charge of Pennilee, Glasgow. That was an appropriate gesture because the parliamentary churches such as Ulva were built, as Church Extension charges were, to serve areas where the populations had greatly increased.

The inside walls and ceiling were plastered and paint-ed, and in the ceiling there were two circular moulded openings for ventilation. The gangways between the pews were simply planks of wood laid on the dry earthen floor. A fine pine pulpit with an overhead sounding board and a precentor's box attached in front was set between the two windows in the east wall. On either side of the pulpit there were two boxed stalls with tables, the laird's on the right and the manse pew on the left. This meant that we were in full view of the congregation throughout

116

the service; an arrangement that I had reason to regret on one occasion.

My father kept, locked up in the press in the study, 'the scissors'. Apart from a small pair that my mother used for sewing, they were the only pair designated by the definite article and they were not for the use of small boys. One Sunday morning, however, when the rest of the family were making ready for church, I was left to my own devices and, spotting 'the scissors', I succumbed to the temptation of playing with the forbidden instrument. After a few tentative snips at scraps of paper I decided to attempt a more ambitious experiment and took a few snips at my forelock. With more enthusiasm than skill I continued until my forelock was reduced to a series of tufts interspersed with bare patches. The family were by this time ready to go to church and I was faced with the daunting prospect of appearing in full view of the congregation displaying my unusual tonsure. Worse still, I would be directly under one of the ventilation openings through which the Almighty kept an eye on proceedings. I grabbed a bonnet and tried to become invisible. Halfway through the first prayer, Mairi, keeping a sisterly eye on me, was scandalised to see that I was wearing a bonnet, contrary to all the proprieties. She snatched the offending headgear off my head, revealing the full extent of my depravity. No thunderbolt descended from the ventilator, but the next day, my father, much amused, composed and sang before the whole household a doggerel lampoon recounting 'The Saga of The Scissors'.

The church was the scene of another incident which I recall with a sense of horror. One Sunday morning, my father and I and Donnie, the fourteen year old son of our neighbours, went over to prepare the church for the noon service. On entering the building we were aware that an intruder had got in before us. It was a wildcat which, on being discovered, became frantic in its effort to escape. Pursued by Donnie, it scrabbled up the smooth, bare plaster walls towards the light of a window seeking a way out. I looked on helplessly, admiring Donnie's courage – wildcats could be savage when cornered – but at the same time devoutly hoping that the cat would elude him and escape. No divine help came via the ventilator, however, and Donnie succeeded in grabbing the unfortunate animal by its allegedly deadly tail and dispatched him against the wall.

No Roman general, returning in triumph from the wars, celebrated his triumph with more éclat than Donnie. 'Spleuch mi ris a' bhall' e!' ('I squashed him against the wall.') To country folk a wildcat posed a threat to domestic poultry and, besides, the pelt of one would fetch a good deal more than a rabbit skin when Barney Long next visited the island.

24

Happier Were We in the Homeland with its Neighbourly Communion and the Bread and Wine of Friendship

THE HEADING OF THIS chapter comes from a poem, 'The Metagama Passes', which appeared in the *Glasgow Herald* over the initials D.B.F. and which describes the feelings of the emigrants who sailed to Canada in the Metagama as they remembered the homeland and the homely and simple celebration of Communion on Sacrament Sunday. The calendar of the West Highlands Christian year, it could be said, had but one red letter day – the once-a-year Communion Sunday held in summer. The Thursday preceding it was the fast day when normal work was suspended and a preparatory service was held in church.

For days before Communion, my mother and helpers were busy preparing the house for the festive occasion. Cutlery was polished, dishes and tablecloths cleaned and chickens prepared for the pot. While the activities in the kitchen reached fever point, we helped our father prepare the church. The long communion table was spread with 'fair linen', a quatern loaf of Yule's bread was decrusted and cut in a special way so that the slices could be broken off for distribution at 'the breaking of bread'. The wine, Cockburn's Fine Invalid Port, was decanted into the flagon and cup, the rich, fruity bouquet filling the building.

During the service, after the sermon, a psalm or paraphrase was sung, during which the communicant members left their pews and took their places around the table, presenting their tokens to the elders. The entire service, including the dispensing of the elements, was conducted by the assisting minister; the minister of the parish was served along with the members of his congregation. The children and those who were not communicant members remained in their pews throughout, sharing and observing but not actively participating.

On one occasion, the visiting minister at communion was the Rev. Dr Archibald MacDonald, minister of Kiltarlity, a distinguished Highland genealogist, prose writer and collector of Gaelic poetry. He was staying at Gometra in the house of his sister, Flora, the wife of the laird of Gometra, Roderick Maclean. At the close of the service he stood at the door of the church with my father greeting the skailing congregation. One finely arrayed lady with a splendid hat engaged him in polite conversation, and when she left he turned to my father and asked who the fine lady might be. 'She is the lady', my father told him, 'who has been looking after your welfare for the past week.' She was the cook and housekeeper of his sister's house.

Those who had come a long distance to attend communion were invited to stay for dinner at the manse. The dining table could be extended by the insertion of a leaf to accommodate about eight or nine guests. Sometimes there was no room at the table for the children, in which case we either sat at a small table in a corner of the dining-room or at the kitchen table.

The menu never varied from year to year. The first course was chicken soup brought to the table in a large tureen and served by my mother with a ladle. When pressed to partake of the soup, the polite response of the ladies was, 'Half a ladle if you please.' The choice for main course was between roast beef, usually the gentlemen's choice – 'The roast beef of merry England,' Alasdair MacDonald would declare – or boiled chicken with oatmeal and leek stuffing and white parsley sauce, the ladies' choice – 'A small wing, if you please,' they would modestly ask for. Boiled potatoes and other vegetables from the garden were served with the main course, and when invited to have second helpings, the ladies would say,' I have had an ample sufficiency, thank you.' Although all present were Gaelic speakers, the conversation throughout the meal was in English, and these conventional polite phrases were borrowed from another culture and an earlier age. I thought it all very grand and genteel.

The highlight of the meal, as far as I was concerned, was the dessert course – quivering moulds of red and green jellies, Bartlett's tinned pears, whipped and pouring cream. Like Communion itself, this particular dessert course came only once a year. After the meal, tea, never coffee, was served from the wedding tea-service and china, with biscuits and cakes and Alasdair MacDonald would begin the ritual of filling his pipe, cutting the tobacco, rubbing it in the palm of his hand, tamping it carefully into the bowl of his pipe; but he would never dream of lighting up until my mother invited him to do so – the hallmark of a duin' uasail!

The simple and homely West Highland Communion

service, held once a year, reflected the joyful celebration, of the Passover, also the main Festival of the Jewish year, in the context of which the Last Supper was instituted. The Gaelic psalms sung at a Communion service were portions taken from the group of Psalms 113–118 which in Hebrew was known as the Hallel and which was sung as a hymn during the Passover celebrations. 'And when they had sung an hymn, they went out into the Mount of Olives.' The traditional Gaelic Communion psalms were Psalm 116: 'I'll of salvation take the cup,/on God's name will I call.' and Psalm 118: 'This is the day God made, in it/we'll joy triumphantly.' The simplicity of language and lack of ornate ritual of the island observance was a more faithful recreation of the scene of the Last Supper in the Upper Room as described in the Gospels, and the Communion dinner which I have described retained the tradition of the agape, the 'love-feast' or common meal associated with the eucharist of the Apostolic Church.

It was on one such Communion Sunday that an incident occurred that was long remembered by the people of Ulva. My brother Stewart, who was about three years old at the time, had long, fair, curling hair which his mother would not allow to be cut. On that Sunday, amid all the bustle of the occasion, the meal had ended before it was noticed that Stewart was not present. Those at the dining-room table assumed that he was in the kitchen, and those in the kitchen assumed that he was in the dining-room. He had been gone about two or three hours before the search began. A search party was organised and each member was given an area to cover. My remit was to search the shore at the foot of the glebe. On my way there I encountered Percy the cat sunning herself on a shelf of rock and in an amiable mood. I explained to her that I was on an urgent mission and that I had no time to stop and pay attention to her. Older searchers went further afield, through the woods, along the shores, up the braes, until one of them (Donnie MacNeill or Colin Fletcher) caught a glimpse of the unmistakable fair curls bobbing up and down in the thick growth of bracken fronds – in Ulva the bracken grew to a height of six feet – and carried him home on his shoulder. Evidently a sheep had got into the manse grounds through a gate inadvertently left open, and Stewart simply followed it for a mile or so until he was located. He was ravenous when he arrived home, and since there was little left of the dinner, a tin of Fray Bentos corned beef was specially opened for him. My most vivid memory of the event is of Stewart attacking the meat with his bare hands and wolfing it down like a savage, in complete contrast to the genteel table manners of the earlier meal.

25

Weddings, Festivals, High Days and Holidays

Aʟᴛʜᴏᴜɢʜ Cᴏᴍᴍᴜɴɪᴏɴ Sᴜɴᴅᴀʏ ᴡᴀs the only red letter day celebrated within the confines of the church building, there were other ordinances, festivals high days and holidays that were observed by the community in their homes and neighbourhood. The sacrament of baptism was administered, not in the church, but in the home of the parents, and funeral services were conducted at the home of the bereaved family and at the graveside. Weddings, too, were solemnised and celebrated in the bride's parent's homes with neighbours from all over the area present. The ordinances of the Church were not restricted to church of stone and mortar; the Church was anywhere in the parish where people and minister gathered for a religious observance.

In 1987 when Michael Leng, ferryman, married Karen Smith, it was the first wedding ever to take place in Ulva church in its 160 years' existence. I was never at a wedding when I was a boy in Ulva, and so I have to rely on press cuttings to describe what wedding ceremonies were like in those days. The first wedding conducted by my father took place on Wednesday, 3rd July 1918, little more than a month after his induction to the parish. The notice in the *Oban Times* reads:

McVicar – Shanks. At the Schoolhouse, Ulvaferry, Mull, on Wednesday 3rd July, by the Rev. D.W. MacKenzie, assisted by Rev. A. Morrison, Salen, Angus McVicar, 9a Esplanade, Greenock, (son of the late Captain McVicar, Greenock) to Christie Davidson Macleay, eldest surviving daughter of Alexander and Mrs Shanks (Headmaster, Ulva Public School.)

Another undated news item from the *Oban Times* describes a typical Mull wedding of this period that took place in Glenforsa. My father often conducted services outwith his own parish during vacancies. The report, I think, is worth quoting in full:

Glenforsa. A pretty wedding was solemnised at Bentala, Glenforsa, on the 11th March, which created no little stir in and around the glen, it being the first marriage performed in that part of the glen for close upon one hundred years. The contracting parties were Mr Donald Maclean, Gaoideil, and Miss Margaret Mackenzie, Glentala. The officiating clergyman was Rev. D.W. Mackenzie, parish minister of Ulva. The bride was given away by her father, and looked well in a smart white silk frock with a veil of orange blossoms. Miss Effie Campbell, Balthzouk [? Balthayock], Perth, was bridesmaid. Mr N. Maclean, brother of the bridegroom, acted as best man. The large company of guests were drawn from nearly every glen in Mull, and the bridal party were piped up to Glentala cottage. The glen, circled with the high hills of Mull, was bathed in a flood of sunshine, and presented an animated scene. The enchanting sounds of the pibroch cast the echo among the mountains, and the scent of the bogmyrtle perfumed the air. It was truly a lovely scene. A splendid feast was provided by the bride's parents, and after toasts had been proposed and responded to, the party resorted to the lawn for a dance to the strains of the bagpipes, the piper being Mr Angus Livingstone, keeper, Gruline. Mr John Cameron, Salen, one of the ablest fiddlers in Mull, supplied violin music for the Country Dances.

I think that marriage services were conducted in English – the language of authority and officialdom – even when all the parties were Gaelic speakers. At another wedding conducted by my father in Mull, not in his own parish, when he asked the couple to join hands, the groom extended his hand to his bride-to-be and loudly and formally greeted her in English with 'How do you do?' There does not survive in oral tradition much, if any, of a Gaelic order of service for Marriage. Perhaps one anecdote relating to a wedding that took place in Harris in the eighteenth century may provide a hint of what such an order might have contained. According to the anecdote the following exchanges between the minister and the groom took place:

> Minister: Is this woman your one and only choice of all the women in the world?
> Groom (with more candour than tact): She is not, by your leave, Minister. I would rather the daughter of the Tacksman of Berneray if I could have her.

The question put by the minister (in Gaelic: 'An i seo d'aon roghainn de mhnathan an t-saoghail?') has a fine liturgical ring to it, reminiscent of the phrase in the order for marriage in the Church of England's *Book of Common Prayer*, 'forsaking all others'. An Order for Marriage appears in the *Gaelic Supplement to the Church of Scotland's Book of Common Order* (1940), which is simply a translation of the order in English. In the Gaelic section of the archives of the Isle of Mull Museum there are five pages of a small notebook written in small, neat handwriting of a similar version of the marriage service. There is no indication as to who wrote it or when it was written.

Easter and Christmas were not celebrated by special services in church as they are in most churches in Scotland today. That is to say, that the commemoration of the resurrection and the nativity was not tied to particular dates in a calendar. Easter and Christmas were eagerly awaited children's festivals. At Easter relations and friends sent us chocolate Easter eggs; at Christmas they sent us Christmas cards with celluloid transparent panels and parcels containing books, toys, games, paints, crayons and sweets. It was a time when apples and sweets mysteriously appeared in unusual places and when strange footprints of enormous size appeared in the snow if a snowfall coincided with the festive season. We hung up our stockings near the fireplace and in the cold, dark Christmas morning, half asleep but in a fever of anticipation, we pulled out little wooden and tin toys, games, an orange and an apple. At home we sang Christmas carols – 'O come all ye faithful' and 'Child in a manger', the English version of the Mull Carol composed by Mary MacDonald, 'Leanabh an àigh'.

At Christmas, on birthdays and other special occasions

my mother would make a large, fruit steamed pudding – we called it a dumpling, made, not in a cloth like the 'clootie dumpling' but in a large bowl with the top covered with muslin and placed in a large pot of water and boiled for several hours. Flour, sugar, suet, spices, sultanas and I know not what else went into the recipe to produce a rich, satisfying meal in itself when served hot. When cold it was sliced and eaten like a cake and any left-overs could be fried.

By Hogmanay, houses had to be cleaned and tidied and all accounts had to be settled. At the stroke of midnight doors and windows were to be opened to let the Old Year out and the New Year in. On New Year's Day neighbours visited each others' houses, the first-foot, preferably a dark-haired male, presented the housewife with a bit of coal or black bun. The traditional greeting was 'Bliadhna mhath ùr' and the response was 'Mar sin dhuit fhéin is móran dhiubh.' ('A good New Year; the same to you and many of them.') The songs which were practised in the weeks leading up to New Year were sung, and drams were drunk. New Year's Day was a holiday. The season of the year was called in Gaelic a'Challainn (the first day of a month) and Hogmanay was called Oidhche Challainn (New Year's Eve) a time when, in my father's boyhood in Lewis, young men went guizing and repeated traditional rhymes, demanding items of food from the housewives.

At Hallowe'en (Oidhche Shamhna) we played games: dooking for apples and various divination games. We dipped our spoons into a large dish of mashed potatoes in which various small objects were buried. If a girl got a ring it meant she would marry; if a thimble she would remain an old maid. A boy finding a threepenny bit would become a rich man, but finding a button meant that he would always be a bachelor. Apple skins were peeled off in one piece and thrown over the left shoulder. When it landed on the floor it took the form of a letter which would be the initial of your partner to be. You put two hazelnuts side by side in the glowing embers, one representing yourself and the other an imaginary partner. You watched closely to see what would happen when they exploded with the heat: if they were driven closer to one another it augured well for the partnership; if they were driven apart, the partnership was doomed.

In our belief system, Christian and pagan beliefs sat easily alongside each other; the worldly and otherworldly merged and the line between the natural and the supernatural was blurred. Anna Dhubh's cure for Lena, described earlier, is a classic example of this merging and blurring; the stories about fairies and the Each Uisge were other examples that were comfortably accommodated within our view of life and the world – a view more compatible, I think, with that of St Columba and the Celtic Church than that of John Knox and the Church of the Reformation.

26

Travel, Lines of Communication and Postal Services

THE OPENING OF THE Oban Railway in 1880 and improved steamer services opened up lines of communication between the Lowland cities and isolated areas like Ulva. We had the little motor vessel, the *Lochinvar*, that plied daily, except on Sunday, between Tobermory and Oban, calling at ports in between – Drimnin, Salen, Lochaline and Craignure. At Drimnin and Craignure, where there were no suitable piers, she was met by rowing boats that took on or off passengers and cargo. She had capacity for carrying four cars, which were driven on or off across two planks. Instead of a convenional funnel placed amidships, she had four narrow buff-coloured exhaust pipes arranged along the port and starboard sides. The saloon on the upper deck had pictures on its bulkheads illustrating Scott's poem 'Young Lochinvar', which we greatly admired when we were taken to the saloon to have tea, biscuits and red cheddar cheese during the crossing. The captain of the *Lochinvar* then was the well-kent skipper, Captain Black, whose people originally came from Ulva and moved to the Ross of Mull.

Among the archives of the Isle of Mull Museum there are photocopies of newspaper reports and correspondence that trace the subsequent history of Salen pier and the *Lochinvar*. The state of Salen pier was giving concern from the 1940s onward until Argyll County Council decided in October 1960 to upgrade the pier at Craignure to replace Salen as the principal port of call on the Oban-Tobermory run. A newspaper cutting, dated 8th April 1963, reports the closure of Salen pier. The first vessel to operate the new service was the *Lochearn*.

The *Lochinvar* underwent a refit in which the narrow exhaust pipes were replaced by a single buff-coloured funnel of the conventional type. There is a picture of the revamped *Lochinvar*, renamed the saloon ship *Anzio*, in the *Oban Times* (undated) with the caption:

> **Still Going Strong**
>
> Although *Lochinvar* has gone out of the west, the old lady is still showing her mettle! The MacBrayne veteran of the Mull – Oban run is now plying in southern waters – to be exact, out from Southend pier from which she is seen sailing on one of her daily excursions (vide notice board) with buff-coloured funnel, fully licensed refreshment bars and a new name – the saloon ship *Anzio*.

The notice board, pictured, shows the the places visited in the excursions – Sheerness, Warships' Floating Dock, World's Largest Oil-tankers, Isle of Grain Oil Refineries. Fare 4/–.

The tragic end of the *Anzio* is reported in the *Daily Mail* of April 4, 1966, a photocopy of which is in the Isle of Mull Museum archives. The front page shows a picture of the wrecked Anzio fast aground with giant waves sweeping over her. Over the photograph is the headline, 'Shipwreck ten die in gale'. Details of the wreck are given on other pages. 'Ten men died in gale-driven seas that wrecked their 216 ton, 152 ft long coaster *Anzio I* on a sandbank early yesterday – with help and safety less than a mile away. Three more men may be missing.'

The *Anzio* left Tilbury for Scotland on the night of Friday, 1st April. Hit by Saturday's gale she headed for the Humber estuary and struck a rock-hard sandbank a mile off shore. Coastguards, the Humber lifeboat and rocket life-saving volunteers responded to her distress signals. The team waded to within 500 yards but were unable to reach the wreck with the lifeline rockets. She was beginning to break up by the time the lifeboat arrived and shortly afterwards the ten men began to be washed ashore. All wore lifejackets. All were dead. Among the dead were the captain, Adam Fotheringham, aged thirty-seven, Burnbank Terrace, Oban, and his brother, Harold, aged thirty-one.

In our time, the mail from the south, including newspapers, was brought by the *Lochinvar* to Salen and sorted at the Aros post office there. Aros was the postal district which included Ulva and Ulvaferry. Our address was The Manse, Ulva, by Aros. The mail for our district was collected by Sandy Black, the mail contractor, and mail for Gribun and the Ross of Mull by Johnny Cameron. Sandy Black, Oskamull, took over the mail contract from his predecessor who lived at Laggan and for whom he drove the pony and trap that conveyed the mail to and from Salen. By 1924, Sandy was the mail contractor and, instead of using a pony and trap to transport the mail, he used a motor car. He was the first person in the district to have a car for hire – a black Ford tourer with a canvas hood. The car he used for the mail run was also a Ford, Model T, with the body reconstructed into a wooden van with compartments for seating passengers and for the mailbags. The car registration letters for Argyll at that time were SB – his initials, Sandy Black solemnly assured us.

He left Ulvaferry at about 5 a.m. with the outgoing mail and returned with the incoming mail at 6 o'clock in the evening. The letters, cards and parcels were then taken by the postmen on bicycles and delivered to Ulva and Gometra in the dark, often wet and stormy, evenings between 6 and 9 p.m. The Ulvaferry notes in the *Oban Times* for 19th January, 1924, contains an item highly appreciative of the postal service:

> **Postal** – During the war and until quite recently the postal service was curtailed in the district to four days a week, but happily a daily delivery has been resumed, for which the public feel most grateful. The new motorcar put on the road by Mr Alexander Black, the mail contractor, is proving a great boon alike to passengers and the public generally. Mr Black's venture is deserving of the patronage of the whole community. Mr Hugh MacNeill, our energetic postman, pursues his calling with the tenacity of a hardy Celt, and in storm or calm never misses his arduous journey to Gometra on three days a week. Verily the grit and stamina of some of our West Highland rural postmen well deserve the adjective Herculean.

Hugh (Eóghan) the post was succeeded by his brother Lachie. They wore uniforms of navy blue with red piping and round hats with high crowns and with patent leather skips, fore and aft. In wet weather they wore long waterproof capes and leggings. They carried their satchels or mail bags on a carrier fixed in front under the handlebars of their red bicycles. The capes were sufficiently voluminous to cover the entire upper part of their bodies and also their arms and hands and the mailbags strapped to the carriers. A postman thus clad riding his bicycle resembled nothing as much as a tent on wheels. The carbide-acetylene lamp which would have been obscured had it been mounted in the usual place was mounted on a bracket low down on the right hand fork of the front wheel.

I remember Lachie better than I remember Hugh. He would let himself in by the back door, make his way along the cement-floored lobby, through the hall and into the study where we waited, especially at Christmastime, with eager anticipation while he tipped the contents of his bag on to the floor and handed out the cards and parcels to each of us individually according to the address on the covers. After he left, if the weather was wet and stormy, there were pools of water on the waxcloth floor covering, on the concrete passage and everywhere where the rainwater cascaded from his cape.

The opening gambit of conversation never varied:

My father: 'De do naigheachd?' ('What's your news?')

Post: 'Chan eil naigheachd idir agam.' ('I have no news at all.')

My father: 'S math an naigheachd a bhi gun naigheachd idir.' ('No news is good news.')

Lachie was a cheerful, humorous and good-humoured character, a leading light in all the social gatherings of the community. The description of his brother Hugh given above, could equally apply to him.

Urgent messages were passed on, before the advent of the telephone, by telegrams. Ulvaferry Post Office was also a telegraph office, and schoolboys were employed as telegram boys to deliver the decoded message written with an indelible pencil on coarse, buff-coloured paper and enclosed in an orange-coloured envelope. Lachie Beag, for instance, was given the day off school and paid half a crown (2/6 old money) for delivering telegrams to the big house of Gometra. 'Reading the telegrams' became a ritual part of wedding celebrations performed by the best man. Many of those greeting telegrams were in Gaelic – Gaelic so mutilated in the course of trans-mission as to render it incomprehensible.

The roads in Mull were narrow, metalled and surfaced with fine gravel and dust. Stretches of road were allocated to designated roadmen who filled in pot-holes and cleared the ditches at the roadsides. I do not remember seeing any tarred road. The roads were quite adequate for the traffic they carried. Cars were few; lairds, doctors, hotel keepers, businessmen owned cars. The Rev. Neil MacPhail, Bunessan, was the only minister I remember driving a car. The bicycle was the commonest mode of transport. I learned to cycle on my father's bicycle by perching on the saddle and launching myself down a small slope near the church and pushing the pedals as they came up to reach my feet.

The first time I visited Iona was when my father was assisting the parish minister, the Rev. Archibald MacMillan at the Communion in the parish church. On the way home, at a corner of the road somewhere between Fionnphort and Bunessan, the car we were riding in, Sandy Black's Ford tourer, collided with the car driven by the hotel keeper at Iona, also called MacKenzie. As both cars were travelling at about 10 mph the impact was minimal and we continued, unscathed, on our respective homeward journeys. It is not unlikely that ours were the only cars using the stretch of road between Fionnphort and Ulvaferry that Sunday evening.

Most families living near the sea had boats. Captain Compton of Torloisg and Roderick Maclean of Gometra had motor launches. The latter also had a gig or trap – we called it a 'machine' – and a groom to drive it. But no-one went to the length of my father's immediate predecessor, the Rev. John Stewart, minister of Ulva from 1913 to 1917, who built his own boat. During the building of it he erected round it a sort of shelter, and by the time the building was completed the boat had outgrown its shell which then had to be demolished to release it for launching. With some humour, the minister named his vessel *The Wide, Wide World.*

He set sail in it for Tiree, (I think that was his native island) accompanied by Mr Alexander Shanks, schoolmaster at Ulvaferry from 1900 to 1919. They ran into a storm at the Treshnish Isles and fear for their safety was aroused. The famous naturalist, Seton Gordon, on coastguard patrol in Gometra raised the alarm but the intrepid mariners turned up safe and sound back in Ulva. In 1917 John Stewart, minister/boatbuilder, was translated to Tiree, an island renowned for its export of famous ministers and skippers.

27

Summer Visitors to Ulva

WHEN SUMMER CAME TO our little island it brought with it delights which defy description – sights and sounds and scents that linger in the memory long after the five senses, so keen in boyhood, have become dulled – the call of the cuckoo, the rasping crake of the corncrake, the humming drone of the flying beetle; the flash of the yellowhammer's wings, the iridescent blue of darting dragonflies; the sweet scent of primroses, the subtle delicate fragrance of wild hyacinths on the woodland floor after a summer shower, the sharp sweetness of the little red and white dog-roses; the smell of newly-mown hay, of bogmyrtle and wild thyme.

And summer, too, brought visitors to our shores to add new interests and pleasures to our lives – friends and relatives who stayed with us for a few weeks, and casual visitors from other parts of Mull who spent an afternoon or evening with us.

One regular summer visitor I remember was the policeman from Salen who came to the island, I think, to ensure that the mandatory sheep-dipping procedures were duly carried out. He called at the manse by way of a courtesy call and I remember him, a large, stolid, dignified pillar of the Law, clad in a tunic with silver buttons fastened up to his throat, sitting upright at the study table, talking to my father in English and partaking solemnly of a large jug of milk and scones that my mother set before him. I imagine that he was the conscientious kind of policeman who would nightly fill in his notebook with details of his daily duties – 'I proceeded on my bicycle in a southerly direction to Ulva . . .' I imagine that he rarely, if ever, had to report any criminal offence.

Another regular summer visitor was the Rev. John M. Menzies, Tobermory, a Perthshire man who spoke Perthshire Gaelic. He was Clerk to the Presbytery of Mull and entered his minutes in the minute book beautifully illuminated. He came accompanied by his wife and daughter. His wife, Mrs Emma L. Menzies was well-known as the writer of the books under the title 'News from Adhachlachair', humorous accounts of country life in the Highlands based on her own experiences of life in Highland manses. Later, she was to write for radio's 'Children's Hour'.

I also remember visits from Mr Langton, the exciseman in Tobermory with his wife and daughter. He was a large, bluff, affable Yorkshireman with an accent barely comprehensible to us children and with a loud, booming laugh that echoed around the hills. On one visit, he asked me how old I was and when I told him that I would be eight on my next birthday he asked when that would be and what I would like as a birthday present. When I took in what he was asking, my mind conjured up various objects of desire. I used to watch the older men filling and lighting their pipes – pipes with straight stems, with curved stems, some with silver mounting, pipes with different shapes of bowl – these were the most desirable objects I could think of. That was it.'A pipe,' I blurted out. You could have heard the bellow of laughter this unexpected response evoked from our visitor had you been standing at the Eas Fors, but several months later when my birthday arrived, a parcel arrived for me by post from the gauger, not a tobacco pipe, admittedly, but a set of building blocks with pictures on them that I treasured for many a long day.

It was not the only time that visitors to our shores sent me a surprise parcel. My father kept a diary in which he entered daily happenings and financial transactions, and when I was given a small notebook with a glossy black cover I decided to emulate his example. Whereas his diaries, had they survived, would have furnished full and exact details of daily events throughout the years, my idea of keeping a diary was to write the day and date and underneath enter anything, however trivial and commonplace, that occurred in it. On the back pages, under the heading 'Cash', I recorded the threepenny bits and sixpenny bits that visitors gave me from time to time. As there were no shops in the area pocket money for children was irrelevant.

I carried this little notebook around with me and one day when playing on the shore I lost it. Some weeks later, Lachie the Post delivered a parcel addressed to Master Donald W. MacKenzie, The Manse, Ulva, by Aros, Isle of Mull. It was not Easter or Christmas nor my birthday when it came, nor had anything been ordered for me from Oxendales. I opened it carefully, untying the knots on the string so that it could be used again and there, inside, was the lost diary and a box of Terry's chocolate.

A letter enclosed explained how members of the Terry family, coming ashore from their yacht while cruising round Ulva, found the diary and how they enjoyed reading it. The box of chocolates was by way of saying 'Thank you.' Also enclosed was a bright, new half-crown piece to add to my bank balance. A half-crown, two shillings and six pence, one eighth of a pound, was, to me, a staggering amount. With it I could have bought the entire stock of chocolate bars in Allan Dally's van: not that I would have done so. It would have been insensitive, to say the least, to spend the Terry bounty on the products of their chocolate manufacturer competitors, Cadbury, Frys and Duncans.

While the family watched in awe as the contents of the parcel were revealed my mother took the opportunity to glance through the diary that earned for me such fame and fortune. She was not well pleased to light upon one entry, the sole entry recorded for one day – 'Mama washed her feet today.'

Other regular visitors to Ulva were the itinerants, such as Peter Braddley who during his stay on the island lived in a cave on the shore opposite our house. He was a small Irishman who spoke Irish Gaelic. He had been, we understood, a seaman and he wore a peaked cap. He carried his wares about in a little wheeled buggy. If we spoke to him we were told to address him politely as Mr Braddley. Similarly, another itinerant, Barney Long, also Irish, had to be called Mr Long. He made his living going round the islands and mainland of Argyll buying, for a few pence, rabbit skins and other pelts that we kept for him. As far as I know, the fur trade was his only business. He was allowed to sleep in our haybarn on condition that he refrained from smoking his pipe in it.

Occasionally we had visits from travelling people who

sold us small items such as clothes pegs and tin cans. One red-haired family whose name I have forgotten made and sold brightly coloured paper flowers which I thought were very fine works of art. The mother assured us that all the children, from the smallest tot upwards, were engaged in the work. 'They're all flower-daft,' she would say and that remained in our family as a kind of catchword for years afterwards.

As the long summer began to merge into autumn and the days grew shorter and cooler, the visitors, like the cuckoo and other migrants, began to depart, leaving us to resume our normal island routine. We were sorry to see them go. Years later, when I lived in Barra, I heard an expression used by the Barra folk that echoed that feeling of regret at summer's close. When the *Lochearn* arrived at Castlebay pier, bringing the summer visitors and the relations exiled in Glasgow, it seemed as if the whole population of the island thronged the pier to welcome them. And then, at the end of summer when the visitors were departing, the pier was crowded with the islanders waving them goodbye until next year and the expression on everybody's lips was:

B'fheàrr leinne gu robh sibh a'tighinn seach a bhi falbh.

We would rather that you were coming instead of going.

28

The Wide, Wide World

ULVA DURING THOSE ELEVEN years was to me the hub of the universe. Visitors came and shared our little world briefly, bringing with them reminders that there was a wider world beyond the boundaries of our parish where things were happening that presaged changes, some exciting, some threatening.

The newspapers, too, brought us news from round the world of the events that were taking place. In the *Glasgow Herald*, which came by post each weekday we read about the exciting discoveries at the tomb of Tutankhamun at Luxor during the excavations carried out by the Earl of Carnarvon and Howard Carter in 1922. We cut out the pictures of the artefacts, including the gold mask of the boy king, that were published in the *Herald* and kept them in a large cardboard box.

We followed eagerly the news of aircraft development and pioneering aviators, and we were thrilled to read about, and see pictures of, the first solo Atlantic flight, Col. Charles Lindbergh's flight in the monoplane, the

Spirit of St Louis, from New York to Le Bourget in 1927.

We also read about the political changes that were happening in the country in the 1920s. In 1924 James Ramsay MacDonald formed the first ever Labour Government of Britain. It fell ten months later but in 1929 he again became prime minister. My father who would not have described himself as Labour politically welcomed the rise of socialism. At general elections he and my mother, often accompanied by me, would cross the ferry and walk amicably together to the polling station at Ulvaferry school. The choice was between the Conservative candidate or the Liberal; there was no Labour contestant for Argyll at that time. He would vote for the Liberal and my mother for the Conservative, the one cancelling the other's vote. The Tory M.P. for Argyll for most of the time I remember was Fred MacQuisten, but all I can recall about him is that he was reported to have worn a suit of tussore silk in summer. In conversation, my father would discuss politics with our neighbours and many of them would agree that, given a choice, they, too, would vote Liberal, but they were concerned that, if they did, Clark would find out and instantly dismiss them! So much for their faith in the confidentiality of the ballot box.

The decade was a time of political unrest – the coal strike, culminating in the General Strike of 1926, 'Red Clydeside'. Those events, though centred far from Ulva, presented a threat to the way of life of the remotest islands of the kingdom, dependent as they were on the unhampered transport of fuel and provisions from the south. 'Red Clydeside' manifested itself visibly before our eyes when the nephew of Bean Chaluim Dhughallaich, a young man of the name MacColl, on holiday from the Clyde shipbuilding yards, raised a large red flag on a prominent hillock on his uncle's croft. He was, we were told, a Bolshevik (we pronounced the word with the stress on the second syllable) and, though I did not know what a Bolshevik was, it and the flag appeared vaguely menacing.

I did not fully realise it at the time but, looking back now, I can see that changes were gradually taking place in our own little world during those years. The mail-order catalogue, as I said, brought the latest fashions of mainland Britain to our doors; tinned fruit and meat and fish from all over the world supplemented our homely, traditional fare; home-made cures and cosmetics were replaced by shop-bought preparations.

We did not have a gramophone but some families had and we could listen to records of bagpipe and accordion music played by the best performers of the land; records made by Harry Lauder and other Scots singers and by Mòd Gold Medal Gaelic singers of the day. Music hall ballads of the 'Gay Eighties and Nineties' had already reached the remote Islands of the West, and now the music of Tin Pan Alley and American Ragtime was introduced by the young people who had gone to the Lowland towns to work or to study. Mairi, who had gone to a school in Edinburgh, returned home for holidays and taught us the current hits of the day – 'Felix kept on walking', 'Horsey, keep your tail up' and such gems. The first talking pictures were shown in 1928, and soon the numbers of the great Hollywood musicals appeared in the sheet music that was so popular in the 1930s.

It was at this time, too, that the new wonder of the age was beginning to become popular – the wireless. The first wireless I ever listened to, the first in the parish, was one belonging to Roderick Maclean of Gometra. He invited us to his house to hear it. We, the three boys, were dressed in our kilts for the occasion, and he sent his splendid equipage, his horse and trap, driven by his groom, Cleaver, to fetch us. We were hospitably received by the laird and his lady and then we sat in the drawing-room and waited with bated breath while our host twiddled the knobs of the set. Then strange sounds were picked up from the atmosphere, sometimes obliterating the voices and music that emanated from the little box. It was awesome to sit in that drawing-room in Gometra and listen to voices and music that originated hundreds of miles away with no visible link between the source and the receiver. I personally thought that the wireless was a poor substitute for the gramophone and I doubted if it would catch on, but it was a great day, a day to remember. I still have a photograph of the laird and his lady with us taken outside in the garden to commemorate a very special occasion. The year was 1925.

Near the pier at the Mull side of the ferry there was an old coachhouse which, when I remember first seeing it, was dilapidated and doorless. As children we played in it while waiting for Sandy Black's car to take us to Salen. Inside there was a once-splendid coach, broken down and mouldering in decay, that belonged to the first Francis William Clark who bought Ulva in 1835. Some years later we noticed that a good deal of activity was centred on the old building: the coach disappeared, the floor was cemented, the doors replaced and the roof and walls were repaired. On an outside wall a large petrol tank was installed. Alasdair Fletcher, the manager's eldest son, was sent to the south to learn to drive and maintain a car and he came back, splendidly kitted out in the livery of a chauffeur: navy-blue double-breasted jacket, breeches, black leather spats and a peaked cap, with the Laird's new car – a maroon-coloured Ford saloon.

Ulva was being embraced by the wide, wide world and was in the process of being brought into the twentieth century. The wide, wide world was calling me and beckoning me away from my little world and, I suppose, I was ready to go. When I crossed the ferry to go to Oban High School in 1929, I may not have fully realised that an epoch in Ulva's history was coming to an end. Ulva, I thought, would still be the same when I returned home for the school Christmas holidays in a few months' time. In the event, forty-two years were to elapse before I next set foot on Ulva. On 3rd December 1929 my father was translated to the parish of Kilmelford and Kilninver, bringing a hundred years of Ulva parish church to a close. When I visited Ulva in 1971, the island, indeed, had changed little in outward appearance but of the people living there at that time there was not one I knew in 1929.

Postscript

A T 2.30 ON THE afternoon of Wednesday, 2nd June
1971 I crossed the ferry to Ulva for the first time
since leaving it some forty-two years earlier. With me was
Eric Cregeen, School of Scottish Studies, Edinburgh
University, who was recording Gaelic tradition-bearers in
Mull at that time. Lady Congleton had then been the
owner of Ulva for the past twenty-six years, and no-one
was allowed to land on her island without her express
permission. As we waited at Ulvaferry school for a phone
call confirming her assent to our request for entry, we
passed the time talking to the teacher, Mrs M. Douglass,
and her pupils. There were fourteen on the School Roll,
six of them from the Island of Ulva, some bearing
familiar names of families I remembered, MacFadyens,
MacColls. Not one of them spoke Gaelic.

When eventually we landed on Ulva we were met at
the pier by Mr MacPhail (I do not recall his first name),
with Oban and Kerrera connections, who had been
manager of the estate for the previous nine years. He

took us in a Land Rover on a tour round the haunts that
were once familiar to me: the old steadings that incorporated the remains of the last MacQuarrie chief's old
house; the wall-lined road (The Avenue) leading from
there to the shore; the new steadings (Na Saibhlean ùra);
up the Minister's Walk to the ruins of the old Ulva school,
nearby Ard Airigh, where David Livingstone's father and
grandfather farmed after leaving Uamh (Cave), and,
finally, the church and manse.

Lady Congleton had the church repaired and reconstructed to serve as a community centre, retaining the
restored pulpit, with its sounding-board and precentor's
box, and some of the original pews. In the precentor's
box I picked up a copy of the Authorised Version of the
English Bible and read the words written on the fly-leaf in
clear, confident handwriting:

Francis W. Clark
Writer Stirling
1834

Mr MacPhail kindly let me see through the former
manse, my old home which was now his home and I am
still grateful to him for making me feel so welcome on my
return visit after so long an absence. I was surprised to
find that Ulva had changed so little in the intervening
years; everything, more or less, was as I remembered, but
on closer examination many important changes were
evident. The church and former manse and all the houses
were supplied with electricity from a powerful generator
installed by Lady Congleton and the water supply to the
manse which in our time was piped from a well in Glac
nan Ràmh was piped from a new reservoir. Lady
Congleton built up and improved the stock of cattle and
sheep and introduced modern methods of farm manage-

ment and modern farm machinery, including a sawmill.

In 1980, when Ulva passed to Lady Congleton's heirs, her daughter, the Hon. Mrs J.M. Howard and Mrs Howard's son, Jamie, they continued the work of improvement on the estate and added new industries – salmon and oyster farming and the tourist industry.

My last visit to Ulva on the 8th June, 1992, was arranged for me by my daughter, Ann, who was now living in Mull. She took photographs of the various places on our walk that held memories for me. Walking past the new Ulva House we met the Hon. Mrs J.M. Howard and at Bracadale we called in on Jean Ann MacFarlane who was a little schoolgirl in Gometra when I was a boy in Ulva and who was living in the house where Rob Munro stayed then. Passing the New Steadings we went on to the old church and manse, the latter occupied by the Thomason family who very kindly, like MacPhail, the manager, twenty-one years previously, let me look round their home which was once mine.

At the ferry there was evidence of a new development instituted by the new owners. The old shed beside the ferry house had been renovated and made into the Boathouse Visitor's Centre and another storey added to accommodate a tearoom. An attractive illustrated booklet, *The Isle of Ulva, A Visitor's Guide*, by J. Howard and A. Jones, gave an outline of Ulva's history and described the various walks, all sign-posted, that visitors were free to roam as they explored the island. Overseas visitors, including MacQuarries whose forebears came from Ulva, have held reunions and have been warmly welcomed.

As we returned across the ferry at the end of a glorious summer's day I thought about what I had seen and heard and remembered from the past. Ulva had shown its sunny, smiling face and wore its summer mantle of leafy trees and burgeoning bushes. The air was redolent of bogmyrtle and the little white and red dog-roses and was sharpened by the salty tang of sea and shore. The voices and laughter of children mingled with the call of the sea birds, with the diapason of Eas Fors in the background.

And other ghostly voices and music wafted across the water and across the years – a Rankin piper playing the secret tune, 'A' Ghlas Mheur', he learned from the fairies at the Sìthean of Laggan, the Duke playing 'fragments' on the pampered Lucy, the great pipe-major playing his magnificent, full-silver-mounted bagpipes at Oskamull and Calum Dùghallach calling his cow home for the evening milking from Croit Phàraig a' Chaolais, 'Bó Lilidh. Bó Lilidh. Bó Lilidh!' And, flitting around the periphery of memory and not quite coming into focus, the image of a little bare-footed boy with a dosan, playing on the shore, in the woods, among the rocks; herding the cow, making hay in the glebe, fishing in the boat; listening to songs and stories and the talk of grownups.

Past and present, the quick and the dead, the real and imaginary merged and mingled in that golden summer day in Ulva. Ulva had a past, sometimes tragic, sometimes heroic; I dare to hope from what I saw and heard that day, that Ulva, on the threshold of the new millennium, has a bright future.

Appendix I
Poetry Composed by Ulva People or About Ulva

MOLADH ULBHA Le Cailean Fletcher

Colin Fletcher, son of the manager, gave this song to Ann MacKenzie. Not previously published.

1. Mi nam shuidhe 'n seo leam fhéin
   Smaoinich mi gun innsinn sgeul,
   Na laithean sona bh' agam fhéin
   Nuair bha mi òg an Ulbha.

2. 'S iomadh àit' san do chuir mi cuairt,
   Thall 's a bhos, us sios is suas,
   Chan fhaic mi àit' a dheanainn suaip
   Air eilean luachmhor Ulbha.

3. 'S iomadh latha bh'agam ann,
   A' ruith nan coinnean feadh nan gleann,
   'S gun droch smuaintean na mo cheann,
   Na idir olc no urchair.

4. 'S tric mo smuaintean air Fan Mór,
   Roinn Phort Rainneach, Torr na h-Oa,
   'S mi coimhead null air craobh Dhomhnaill Mhóir
   Far an robh mi aotrom calma.

5. An am an fheasgair b'e mo mhiann
   Bhi dol Phort Sgeireach le seann Niall,
   Toirt nan giomach as a' chliabh
   Bu chiatach a bhi comhl' ris.

6. Ach a nis tha'n aois a' teachd,
   'S bidh mo smuaintean ort gu tric;
   'S iomadh innleachd bha nam bheachd
   Nuair bha mi òg an Ulbha.

7. Ach tha mi'n diugh gu sona, saithe
   Taobh Caol Mhuile 'gabhail tàimh,
   Trusadh maoraich as an tràigh
   Toirt dhomh slàint is sòlais.

PRAISE OF ULVA by Colin Fletcher

1. Sitting here by myself
   I thought I would tell a story
   Of the happy days I had
   When I was young in Ulva.

2. Many a place I visited,
   Hither and yonder, up and down:
   I do not see any place I would exchange
   For the precious Isle of Ulva.

3. Many a day I spent there,
   Hunting rabbits through the glens,
   With no evil thoughts in my head,
   No evil or hurtful thought at all.

4. I often think of Fanmore,
   The parts around Port Raineach, Torr na h-Oa,

Looking across at Big Donald's tree,
When I was light-hearted and confident.

5. At evening time it was my pleasure
   To go to Port Sgeireach with Old Neil,
   Taking the lobsters from the creel –
   It was pleasant to be in his company.

6. But now that age has come
   I often think of you.
   I had many ploys on my mind
   When I was young in Ulva.

7. But today I am happy and content
   Beside the Sound of Mull taking my ease,
   Gathering shellfish from the shore
   Giving me health and solace.

A' BHEINN MHÓR Le Eóghan MacNeill

Previously unpublished poem by Hugh MacNeill, the
Post, given by him to my father.

Séisd: A' Bheinn Mhór an Eilean Mhuile,
       'S a'bheinn bhrèagha o chian na cruinne,
       A' Bheinn Mhór an Eilean Mhuile,
       Os cionn na tuinne cruth 'sa dealbh.

1. Thar Loch nan Ceall 's ann chì mi bhuam thu,
   Currachd gheal ort de'n cheo luaineach;
   'S maiseach thu bho'n linn a fhuair thu
   'N t-urram bhi os cionn a' chorr.

2.   Bho chionn cian tha a' bheinn Mhuileach
Na sealladh àluinn leis gach duine,
'S bidh i siud do'n linn nach d'rugadh
Mar tha i dhuinne 's do na dh'fhalbh.

3.   'S dìreach, cas a tha do stuaghan,
Fuarain chùraidh brùcadh nuas leat;
Biolaireach, bòidheach air an uachdair
Air na cluaintean fuar ri reòt.

4.   Beinn cho gasda 's tha ri fhaotainn,
'S beag dhe d' sheòrsa th'air an t-saoghal;
Ban-righ 'n eilein thu 's gu faod thu –
'S tric an crùn geal cruinn mu d' chròic.

5.   Beinn nan damh donn nan cròic sgaoilteach,
'S tric nan laighe iad 'san fhraoch ort.
Gheibh iad fasgadh air gach taobh dhiot
'N coirichean blàtha fraoich is feòir.

6.   Beinn nam beannachd, beinn mo dhùthcha,
Beinn bho'n d'araicheadh na diùlnaich
Sheasadh blàir nuair theannadh dlùth orr'
Ged tha cuid dhiubh 'n diugh fo'n fhòid.

BEN MORE by Hugh MacNeill

Chorus: Ben More in the Isle of Mull,
            Beautiful ben from the beginning of creation,
            Ben More in the Isle of Mull,
            Your shapely form rises above the waves.

1.   I see you in the distance across Loch nan Ceall
Wearing a white mutch of swirling mist;
Lovely you are ever since you gained
The honour of being above the rest.

2.   From time immemorial the Ben of Mull
          Has been a beautiful sight to all men.
      And so shall it be to generations unborn
      As it was to us and to them who have gone.

3.   Sheer, steep are your peaks
      With fresh springs rushing down them,
      Abounding in cress, lovely on the surface
      On the cold pastures in time of frost.

4.   A ben as splendid as is to be found,
      Few of your kind are in the world.
      You are the queen of the island, as well you may,
      Often the white crown encircles your head.

5.   Ben of the stags of the spreading antlers,
      Often they lie on your heathery slopes.
      They find shelter on every side of you
      In the warm corries of heather and grass.

6.   Ben of my blessing, ben of my land,
      A ben that reared the heroes
      Who would stand firm in battle, though pressed,
      Although some of them now lie under the sod.

Hó MHICCOINNICH Hé MHICCOINNICH
Le John MacGillivray

Séisd: Hó MhicCoinnich, Hé MhicCoinnich,
         Hó MhicCoinnich as Ceann t-Sàile,
         Bho'n latha thàinig thu do'n tìr seo
         Gura mór a thug mi gràdh dhuit.

1.   Nuair a theid thu suas do'n chùbaid
      Nì thu ùrnuigh a bhios àluinn.

'S iomadh neach a rinn thu stiùradh
A null gu cùirtean grinn an Ard-righ.

2. 'S iomadh litir bhàn a sgriobh thu
A chuidich dìlleachdan is màthair;
Fhuair thu portion do na mìltean
'S urram bho'n rìgh 's fo'n a' bhan-righ.

3. Tha thu air Comunn an Fhoghluim
Tha toirt eòl do dh'Earraghaidheal,
'S cinnteach mi gun dean thu feum dhoibh:
Gheibh thu éisdeachd am measg chàich ann.

4. Tha do chéile mar bu dual dhith,
Gu modhail, uasail, suairce, nàrach.
Tha i measail am measg cheudan,
'S thug thu fhéin le spéis do làmhdhith.

5. Chaidh mi gu Pennygail gu dìoblaidh,
Comhla ri Ina 's ri MacPhàidean,
'S bha mo dheas làmh dhuit cho dìleas
'S thug mi sgrìob os cionn MhicPhàil dhuit.

6. 'S lionmhor buaidh a th' ort ri innseadh,
Cha ghabh iad cur sios 's an dàn dhomh.
Tha thu eòlach anns an Fhìrinn,
'S tha thu fìnealt air a' bhàrdachd.

7. B'e mo mhiann bhi fuireach dlùth dhuit,
'S tric ga d' ionndrainn gach latha mi,
Ach nam faighinn trian de m' dhùrachd
Bhithinn nad chùirtean mar a b' àbhaist.

HO MACKENZIE, HE MACKENZIE By John MacGillivray

Chorus: Ho MacKenzie, he MacKenzie
Ho MacKenzie of Kintail!
Ever since you came here
Greatly have I esteemed you.

1.   When you ascend the pulpit
You will offer a beautiful prayer.
Many a one you have guided
Over to the courts of the High King.

2.   Many a white letter you wrote
Which helped widows and orphans.
You secured a portion for thousands
And you were honoured by the king and queen.

3.   You are on the Education Committee
Giving guidance to Argyll.
I am sure you will be of help to them;
You will get a hearing among the rest.

4.   Your wife is as one would expect from her breeding,
Polite, noble, kind, modest.
She is esteemed highly by hundreds,
And you, yourself, gave her your hand with love.

5.   I made my way to Pennygael slowly,
Along with Ena and MacFadyen.
My right hand proved loyal to you –
I gave my pen-stroke to you, not to MacPhail.

157

6.   Many a virtue is told of you.
       I cannot set them all down in my song.
       You are acquainted with Scripture
       And you compose elegant poetry.

7.   It was my desire to live near you,
       Often every day I miss you.
       But were I to get a third of my wishes
       I would be in your courts as of old.

Note: John MacGillivray was manager in Ulva until 1919
       when he went to Balneanach Farm. This previously
       unpublished song composed by him was given to my
       daughter, Ann, a few years ago by one of his
       daughters. It was a song in praise of Rev. D.W.
       MacKenzie, minister of Ulva, 1918–1929 (my father,
       apparently at the time when he was elected a member
       of the Education Authority of Argyllshire (Comunn
       an Fhoghluim, v. 3). In verse 5 the composer describes
       going with Ina (his wife?) and someone called
       MacFadyen to Pennygael and recording his vote in
       favour of my father in preference to another
       candidate called MacPhail. (Was this the Rev. Neil
       MacPhail, minister of Bunessan, at the time?)

GLEN ULVA AIR: O' A' THE AIRTS THE WIND CAN BLAW. By the Rev. D.W. MacKenzie, Minister of Ulva. From the *Smeòrach nan Geug* collection.

'Twas on a misty summer morn
   I wandered in the glen.
By chance I saw the ruined cots
   Of a thousand Highland men;
The cruel, callous Lowland laird

Had made them cross the deep,
And in their stead he filled the dales
   With flocks of Cheviot sheep.

The bracken and the thistle wild
   Are over floor and hearth,
The path that led up to the well
   Is covered o'er with earth;
The knoll on which the infants played
   Is hardly now the same,
Instead of laughing children
   'Tis now the haunts of game.

The barley and potato plots
   Are under swards of green;
The stackyard is a ruin quite,
   No human form is seen.
The moorland thrush so gaily sings
   As in the days of yore,
Its sweetly melodies are lost,
   For men are there no more.

The little churchyard on the brae
   Presents a dismal sight:
Where many a clansman hero rests
   Once valiant in the fight;
The sacred acre is bereft
   Of any dyke or wall.
'Tis burrowed through from east to west
   'Mong nettles wild and tall.

The fiery cross oft raised the ire
   Of many a clansman bold
When news went north that foes were near
   To take his field and fold.

The claymore he would handle deft,
  And fearless face the foe,
And routed home the Lowlanders
  And many were laid low.

When wars arose the call to arms
  Resounded through the glen.
In vain the Empire in her plight
  Called for her Highland men,
But there were few to hear the call
  Save deer and Cheviot sheep:
The men were driven off the land
  And made to cross the deep.

Note: Ulva had at one time a population of 600 inhabitants, but shortly after Clark bought the island he evicted every smallholder within its bounds and demolished the houses. A more cruel deed was never perpetrated in the Highlands. There is not a small-holder on the island now – only a few employees. – *An Smeòrach*

LORD ULLIN'S DAUGHTER By Thomas Campbell (1774–1844)

Verse 2. 'Now who be ye would cross Lochgyle
  This dark and stormy water?'
'O! I'm the chief of Ulva's isle,
  And this, Lord Ullin's daughter.'

This poem has become the best remembered of all Campbell's poems. It formed the essential part of the repertoire of poetry and prose that Scottish schoolboys learned by rote ever since it was published up to the 1930s. It has occasioned much speculation regarding the incident it describes.

Thomas Campbell, born in Glasgow, after graduation from the University there, spent five months in 1795 as tutor with the family of the Campbells of Sunipol in the Mornish district of Mull. The mother of the children, then a widow, was a kinswoman of the poet. He is said to have visited Ulva several times during his stay in Mull. It was some time during this period that he heard the story, or a translation of the story, that was current in Mull at the time which was to be the basis of his poem. It was not, however, completed until 1804, by which date he had gone to live in London. It was eventually published in the same volume as 'Gertrude of Wyoming' and other poems in 1809.

Many writers have put forward theories regarding the location and personae of the tragic event. Among the letters to the *Oban Times* on the subject there is a letter from my father, then at Kilmelford, dated 27th January 1930, in which he summarises the traditions that were current in the district during his time there as follows:

> Mr Clark, Senior of Ulva, when he bought the island about the year 1835 wrote to Thomas Campbell asking for further information regarding the incident of the poem and the poet replied that he knew nothing but what had been related in the poem. Further the story is current, in the district that Lord Ullin's daughter was none else but Lord Allan's daughter, and the poet, taking poetic licence, changed the latter to the former. Laird Allan Maclean was proprietor of Knock at the head of Loch na Keal and the young chief of Ulva was refused Lord Allan's daughter in marriage with the result that the young couple resolved to tread the heather through the high hills on the south side of Loch na Keal to get to Ulva by Gribun . . .

The letter concludes, 'Why, the very graves of the young couple covered over by oblong slabs of stone, are still to be seen on the shore of Loch na Keal at a spot where the bodies were washed ashore.' He does not give the exact location of this spot.

The rock, submerged at high tide, known as Bógha MhicGuaire, half-way between Inch Kenneth and Eilean Eòrsa, is believed to be the reef on which the boat foundered, and the spot where the bodies were washed ashore is believed to be on the Mull shore below Oskamull about a half mile east of the ferry. During its Gathering in Mull in 1985, Clan MacQuarrie dedicated a Celtic cross, mounted on a cairn, with the poem inscribed on it, over the grave. A half acre of ground around the grave is now owned by a member of Clan MacQuarrie. (*A Book about MacQuarries*, ed. Rodney L. McQuary, BD, DD.)

AS I CAME HOME LAST NIGHT Anon.

1.   As I came home last night,
Late home came I.
There in the stable
A saddle horse I spy.
'Whose horse is that, Mother?
Whose can it be?'
'It's only a milking cow.'
My mother says to me.

Refrain: Shiubhail mi is shiubhail mi
'S gach àit 'san robh mi riamh
(Repeated thrice)
A saddle on a milking cow
Chan fhaca duine riamh!

I travelled and I travelled
And in every place I was ever in
(Repeated thrice)
A saddle on a milking cow
No man ever saw!

2.   As I came home last night,
Late home came I.
There in the hallway
A walking-stick I spy.
'Whose stick is that, Mother?
Whose can it be?'
'It's only a porridge-stick.'
My mother says to me.

Refrain: Shiubhail mi is shiubhail mi, etc
A silver-mounted porridge-stick
Chan fhaca duine riamh!

3.   As I came home last night,
Late home came I.
There in the parlour
An overcoat I spy.
'Whose coat is that, Mother?
Whose can it be?'
'It's only a blanket.'
My mother says to me.

Refrain: Shiubhail mi is shiubhail mi, etc.
Buttons on a blanket
Chan fhaca duine riamh!

4.   As I came home last night,
Late home came I.

There in the bedroom
An old man I spy.
'Whose man is that, Mother?
Whose can he be?'
'It's only a baby.'
My mother says to me.

Séisd: Shiubhail mi is shiubhail mi, etc.
Whiskers on a baby
Chan fhaca duine riamh!

Note: I remember hearing this comic English/Gaelic song being sung at the ceilidhs in Ulvaferry schoolhouse. I have never seen it in print. Songs composed in this style, partly in English, partly in Gaelic, so-called macaronic verse, were popular from the eighteenth century onwards. William Ross, one of the greatest of the eighteenth century bards, composed verse in this form.

ORAN FEAR SGALASDAIL Alasdair MacMhuirich
SONG OF THE TACKSMAN OF SCALASDALE A. Currie

Séisd: Hug orann ó robha hó
Mo nighean donn bhòidheach
Hug orann ó robha hó
'S truagh nach robh mi 's mo leannan
Ann an gleannan is ceò ann.
Ann an Sgalasdail bheag chreagach
Far an cinneadh an t-eòrna.
Gur i buidseach Chloinn Ghriogair
A chuir mis' air an tòir oirr'
Dol gam phòsadh air daoraich

'S gun mo ghaol a bhi òg oirr'

Chorus:　Hug orann o robha ho
My bonnie brown-haired girl
Hug orann o robha ho
Alas! that my lover and I
Were not in a little misty glen.
In little rocky Scallasdale
Where barley used to grow.
It is the witch of Clan Gregor
That set me in pursuit of her.
By getting me married while drunk.
Never having loved her in my youth.

Note:　I heard this song sung to my mother by Annie
MacDonald (Anna Dhubh), Acharoinich, when I
was a small boy in Ulva, and many years later I
passed the words and melody on to the Rev. William
Matheson, Department of Celtic, Edinburgh
University, who recorded it with several other
verses for the School of Scottish studies in 1974. It
was published in the school's quarterly magazine,
Tocher, No 17, Spring 1975. The poem is said to
have been composed by Alasdair MacMhuirich
(Currie) who worked for Allan Maclaine, tacksman
of Scallasdale and it is the unhappy love affair of
Maclaine that is recounted by the poet, not his
own. According to Mull tradition, Allan was in
love with the daughter of the factor, Campbell of
Ardnacross but, by the machinations of the
Gregorson 'witch' he was married off to a daughter
of Gregorson of Ardtornish when he was too
drunk to realise what was happening.

Appendix II
The Lost Townships of Ulva

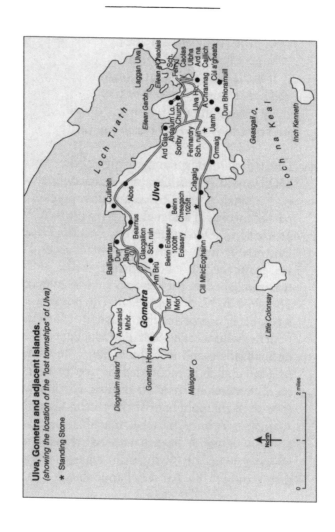

Ulva, Gometra and adjacent islands.
(showing the location of the "lost townships" of Ulva)

★ Standing Stone

Rental for Estate of Ulva for year 1824					Census 1841		1918–29
Names of townships (Alternative sellings)	No. of farms*	Rental £	S	D	No. of houses	No. of people	Houses ruined/ occupied
1. Ormaig	3	104	3	6	8	52	ruins
2. Cragaig	7	67	3	6	10	57	1 family
3. Kilvikewen – Upper (Cill MhicEóghain)	3	52	5	6	8	43	ruins
Kilvikewen – Lower	3	73	15	0			
4. Eolasary	3	66	0	0	6	32	ruins
5. Glacnagallan	5	61	12	0	6	35	ruins
6. Ballygarten (Baileghartan)	4	61	10	0	8	32	ruins
7. Berniss (Bearnus)	5	43	10	9	5	25	1 family
8. Culinish	6	63	18	3	9	52	ruins
9. Aboss (Abas)	5	53	2	0	5	33	ruins
10. Soriby	4	64	7	6	6	29	ruins
11. Ferinardry (Fearann Ard–àirigh)	8	56	14	0	11	54	ruins
12. Ardellum (Ardalum/Ardali)	9	80	3	0	11	46	2 families
13. Salen (Sàilean) Ruadh	1	3	18	6			1 family (Croit Phàraig)
14. Ulva Inn	1	26	0	0			1 family
15. Sound of Ulva (Caolas)	2	22	8	0	6	23	1 family
16. Ard na caillich and							3 families (Bracadale)
17. Cove (Uamh) and Sound of Ulva	Propr.	120	0	0			1 Ulva House
Islands	Propr.	5	0	0			
18. Lagganulva (pt.), Mull Mansion and Garden, ditto	1	86	0	0			2 families
		30	0	0			

* Some farms had joint tenants, father and son, brothers, partners

The total rental for 1824, £1142 11/6, was augmented by the sale of 100 tons of kelp at £6 per ton

Appendix III
Ulva – Etymology of the Name

IT IS GENERALLY ACCEPTED that the name Ulva is of Scandinavian origin, that it is derived from two Old Norse words, *ulfr*, meaning 'wolf' and *ey*, meaning 'island', giving 1) Wolf's Island (a personal name) 2) Wolf Island (from the sea it gave the appearance of a crouching wolf) or 3) Island of Wolves (frequented by wolves).

Ulva is rendered in Gaelic as Ulbha, pronounced OOL-a-VA, three syllables with the middle glide vowel ('a') pronounced but not written. People confronted with words from a language that is unfamiliar to them (e.g. Old Norse) try to make sense of them by substituting similar sounding words from their own language (e.g. Gaelic) and then inventing a legend to explain why the place was so named.

The name Ulva has attracted to it two examples of this so-called 'folk etymology'. In the first, the O.N. *Ulfr-ey* is replaced by the Gaelic *ullamh* (ready) *dha* (to him, for him). Ullamh dha (ready for him) sounds roughly similar to the Gaelic pronunciation of Ulbha. But why should an island be given the unlikely name 'Ready for him'? Because, the legend runs, a scout sent ashore from the Viking long-boat to spy out the land reported back to his chief that the island would not offer resistance and that it was 'Ready for him'.

The other example of this kind of etymology attached to Ulva also uses the Gaelic word *ullamh* (ready) with the Gaelic *àth* (ford). In the OSA Kilninian (Rev. Mr Archibald McArthur) there is a footnote: 'Most names of places are evidently of Gaelic derivation... Ulva, an island separate from Mull by a narrow sound, signifies Ready Ford or Pass.' Ullamh àth is pronounced exactly like Ulbha. No explanation as to why it should be so called is given, but, while not endorsing this fanciful derivation, the following letter to The *Oban Times* may offer a clue:

Ulva's Isle
(To the Editor of the Oban Times)
Manse of Ulva
15 March 1926

Sir,

I have pleasure in replying to the query in Cragaig's letter in your issue of the 13th inst. relative to a paragraph which appeared some time ago in the 'Oban Times' to the effect that there was still living a man in the vicinity who, many years ago at a low ebb, walked across from the mainland of Mull to Ulva's Isle.

The man who did this is Mr Donald MacColl, retired gamekeeper, Ballygowan, Mull. One Sunday morning, he told me, he walked down to the ferry, and noticing the exceptionally low ebb at a point about four hundred yards north of the ferry where the sound is very narrow, he proceeded to walk across, first to a small island in the channel, and from there to Ulva dryshod. He had on a pair of Wellington boots, a style of footgear which was rather fashionable in those days.

I have resided on Ulva's Isle for the past eight years, and being interested in any plan, ebb, road or bridge, to connect me with the mainland of Mull, I eagerly watched the low ebbs to see if it might not be possible for one to walk across; but at no time did I see the tide far enough out to allow one to do so. But it is a well known fact that with strong currents a bar sometimes forms at the entrance of a channel and this gathering of sands and gravel breaks up again with reverse tides. The fact, however, remains that Mr MacColl walked across as stated, and as he is still hale and hearty, he can verify the statement which appeared in the recent issue of the 'Oban Times' that there is still living a man who walked across to Ulva.

The route taken by Donald MacColl in his traverse across the Sound of Ulva via Eilean a' Chaolais was the route (in the opposite direction) over which 'the handsome herds of Ulva were "floated" across the ferry on their way to the Oban sales' as described by Angus Henderson in the article on Ulva in *The Scottish Field*, Sept. 1918, as 'one of the most picturesque incidents in the life of the island'. 'The cattle are driven into the water and forced to swim to a small island. Here they are allowed to rest for a few minutes and then they are made to complete their swim to Mull. Men in boats guide them to the right landing places. This task has to be accomplished twice a year and forms a scene of bustle, excitement and, to the spectator, much romantic interest.'

Bibliography

Attwater, Donald, *The Penguin Dictionary of Saints*, Penguin Books 1965

Boswell, James, *Journal of a Tour to the Hebrides*, London 1785

Caimbeul, Maolios, *A Ulbha gu Geelong*, Acair, Stornoway 1992

Cameron, A.D., *Go Listen to the Crofters*, Acair, Stornoway 1986

Cameron, Alastair, 'North Argyll', Various articles, *The Oban Times*

Campbell, Rev Duncan M., *The Campbell Collection of Proverbs* (ed. Donald E. Meek), Gaelic Society of Inverness 1978

Campbell, John L., *Songs Remembered in Exile*, Aberdeen University Press 1990, Birlinn Ltd, Edinburgh 1999

Commissioners for Building Churches in the Highlands, 6th Report 1830–31

Craig, David, *On the Crofters' Trail*, Jonathan Cape, London 1990

Currie, Jo, *Mull Family Names*, Brown & Whittaker, Tobermory 1998

Devine, T.M., *The Great Highland Famine*, John Donald, Edinburgh 1992

Eckstein, Eve, *Historic Visitors to Mull, Iona and Staffa*, Excalibur Press, London 1992

Fasti Ecclesiae Scoticanae

Henderson, Angus, *Ulva, Argyle, The Scottish Field* Sept 1918

Howard, J. & Jones, A., *The Isle of Ulva, A Visitor's Guide*, Visitor Centre, Ulva 1990

Johnson, Dr Samuel, *A Journey to the Western Isles*, London 1775

McAnna, James, *The Ulva Families of Shotts*, Community Centre, Shotts 1991

MacCormick, John, *The Island of Mull*, Glasgow 1923

Macintyre, Lorn, *Ulva – Island of Memories*, *The Scots Magazine* Sept 1984

MacKay, Rev John, *The Church in the Highlands*, London 1914

MacKenzie, W.C., *The Highlands and Islands of Scotland*, Moray Press, Edinburgh 1937 (rev. 1949)

Maclean, Allan, *Telford's Highland Churches*, Society of West Highland and Island Historical Research, Coll 1989

Maclean, Fitzroy, *A Concise History of Scotland*, Thames & Hudson, London 1970

Maclean, Malcolm and Carrell, Christopher, *As an Fhearann*, Mainstream Publishing, Edinburgh, An Lanntair, Stornoway 1986

Maclean, Charles, *The Isle of Mull. Placenames*, Dumfries 1997

MacLeod, Rev Dr Norman, *Caraid nan Gaidheal*, Inverness 1867

MacQuarrie, Bruce, *Far from their Island Home*, Bruce McQuarrie, Auburn, Mass. USA 1999

McQuarrie, Duncan M., *The Placenames of Mull*, Inverness 1982

McQuary, Rodney L., *A Book about MacQuarries*, Bruce McQuarrie, Auburn, Mass. USA 1989

Monro, Sir Donald, *Description of the Western Isles*, (1549) Edinburgh 1774

Morrison, Neil Rankin, *Clann Duiligh: Piobairean Chloinn Ghill-Eathain*, TGSI, Vol 36 1934

Mull Museum Archive List

Munro, R.W., *Lachlan MacQuarrie XVI of Ulva*, Karachi 1944

Munro, R.W. & MacQuarrie, Alan, *Clan MacQuarrie – A History*, Bruce McQuarrie, Auburn, Mass. USA 1996

Murray, W.H. *The Islands of Western Scotland: The Inner & Outer Hebrides*, Eyre Methuen, London 1973

New Statistical Account, *Kilninian & Kilmore, Argyll*, 1843

The *Oban Times*, Articles, Letters, News items, Oban 1918–29

Old Statistical Account, *Kilninian & Kilmore, Argyll*, 1843

Smout, T.C. *A History of the Scottish People*, London 1969, Fontana 1972

Smout, T.C. *A Century of the Scottish People*, Collins, Fontana, London 1986

Somers, Robert, *Letters from the Highlands on the Famine of 1846*, first published 1848, The Melven Press 1985

Thomson, Derick S. (ed.) *The Companion to Gaelic Scotland*, Blackwell, Oxford 1983

Ulva Estate Papers

Walker, Rev. Dr John Margaret M. McKay (ed.) *Report on the Hebrides 1764 and 1771*, John Donald, Edinburgh 1984